He C

An inspirational true story of different events in my life and the Glory of God's Never-ending Love.

Jehovah Shammah- The Lord is There

[35] *It was round about eighteen thousand measures: and the name of the city from that day shall be, The LORD is there. Ezekiel 48:35*

The Lord who is present. He never leaves you, nor forsakes you. He is with you forever. He is your best friend, who never betrays you.

By Lisa Bryan

He will cover you with His feathers,

under His wings

you will find refuge.

Psalm 91:4

Dedication

This book is lovingly dedicated to my good friend Marilyn Evanisko, whom I call my Angel on Earth.

While I have so many on my list that I could choose, Marilyn is the person my heart has chosen. She is one of my most valuable mentors, and I thank God for the gift of such a wonderful friend.

She has touched my life with love and helped me mature and grow to be a positive spirit-filled woman. She never judged me, and I never heard her speak a harsh word about anyone. With her guidance over the years, I learned that whenever I am feeling sad, lost, or frustrated, that the first call I should make should be to JESUS. I will never get a busy signal, He won't let me get caught up in drama, and I will never get led astray from HIM.

Marilyn, even in her senior years, is truly a mighty warrior for the Lord. Years ago she transported my sons to and from temple every Friday night. Over the years she has transported many both young and old to temple. She accompanied me to every outreach event I participated in. She is on the Prayer ministry, she is always present at the prayer watches, and she is always the first to volunteer to go to the nursing homes and other outreach trips. Her enthusiasm is contagious. She loves to share the Lord with all that she can reach. She often needs to be reminded to sit back and bask in His Presence.

Marilyn, I love and appreciate you!

Acknowledgements

This book was written as an encouraging inspiration for all to read.

First, I give my thanks to God. I said, "Hineni ABBA" (Here I am), and He chose to use me mightily. He gave me the title, the words, and the ambition. He placed the people in my path to assist me along the way. Without my even asking, I had an editor and a partner willing to assist with the cost. This is the way our FATHER works.

Thank you to my husband, Oral, for being supportive of me over the years. We may not travel the world together, but you make it possible for me to continue to be me! Never one to step in my way or say no to my plans, but always there to hold me up when life throws a whirlwind my way. I thank God daily for you in my life.

Thank you to Rabbi Joseph Vitkus, from Temple Aron Hakodesh, for sharing his childlike love of Yeshua with all who will listen and for listening to God when God told Him to show my son love. Because of Rabbi Joe's obedience to the Lord, my sons and I became members of temple and my faith grew from that one seed that was planted. Between Rabbi Joe and our founder Rabbi Neil Lash {who has since passed away}, the endless messages given in TAK taught me and equipped me for a time such as this. I appreciate you both.

Preface

This book is written, not as a reflection of my life, but as a testimony showing the amazing Presence of God in all my circumstances. I pray that by sharing my experiences it may give hope to others whose eyes have not yet been opened wide enough to see that He is ever so present every minute of our lives. When your heart and your eyes are opened, you will be amazed to see how He will swoop in and WOW you with His Mighty blessings of Love, Joy, Strength, Compassion, and Perfect Peace. Nothing is too small for Him to care about. Simply seek God every day and you will see.

> *He will cover you with His feathers, under His wings you will find refuge: **Psalm 91:4***

I've tried many times to share stories about my life but always stopped mid-track, because my stories would flutter from one period in life to another without any type of organization.

One Sunday morning in 2017, I was thinking about how people always tell me I should write a book, since I have been through so much in my life and have great testimonies of God's Presence through it all. I thought of all the other times I tried, and wondered how I could accomplish this task. All of a sudden, the thought came to me, "To write that book you need to start from the very beginning."

Four hours later at a Woman's Worship and the Word meeting, Linda was playing the keyboard and singing when suddenly she blurted out: "Ladies, I want you to write down your life, the good, the bad and the ugly and thank HIM."

That was God's BOLD confirmation that I should indeed write a book. The seed was planted that morning.

I picked up the pen that day determined to write. I knew in my heart that I was supposed write and share the goodness of God with all who would read it. Somehow, I just couldn't seem to get it right. This time I had several chapters with pieces of different stories, but I did not know how to put it together. Once again, I put it on the back burner.

> *Isaac spoke up and said to his father Abraham, "Father?" "Yes, my son?" Abraham replied.*
>
> *"The fire and wood are here," Isaac said, "but where is the lamb for the burnt offering?"* **Genesis 22:7**

In November 2019, I was sitting in church at Pentecostal Tabernacle International in Miami. Pastor S. Robert Stewart was giving a message and he quoted Isaac asking his father where the burnt offering was. His voice got louder as he continued on to say, "PEOPLE, I AM TALKING TO YOU! DO WE HAVE THE FIRE AND THE WOOD BUT NO LAMB? YOU CANNOT JUST COME TO CHURCH EVERY SUNDAY AND LISTEN. YOU NEED TO BRING A SACRIFICE! YOU NEED TO DO SOMETHING FOR HIM, YOU NEED TO DO MORE! WHERE IS YOUR BURNT OFFERING?"

Several people went up to the front and talked about different plans that they had to help in the community, to open a business, and so forth. I began talking to God, "Here I am Lord, wanting to do more for You, please guide me ABBA and tell me what more I can do." I raised my hands to Him and began singing the song the choir was singing. As I stood

9

there singing, memories of different times in my life that He swooped in and rescued me kept popping into my head. Suddenly, "HE COVERS ME" came boldly into my thoughts. I realized I finally needed to put everything to the side and make time to write that book, and that He already chose the title, "HE Covers Me!"

I walked up to the crowded altar to lay the book and all that goes with it down for Him to bless. Yes, Lord, I will do it. I am trusting that You want me to write about You and that you will equip me with the words and with the helpers to edit and publish this book. I will give it my all Lord, for You!

A few days later I was on Claudia Roberts Facebook Live's "Awaken to pray" session. She was talking and praying on many topics. I do not recall the topic we were on when all of a sudden, she blurted out: "IF GOD GIVES YOU SOMETHING TO DO -DO IT."

This was the beginning of the book you are about to read. It is a book to encourage others who are walking in my shoes in one of my many circumstances. He has led me through the waters and carried me when I could not walk. He has covered me from head to toe with a cocoon-like protective covering that keeps me strong when a regular person would lose it or give up -like through a break-up, or the loss of a child.

Through my stories you will see the pivotal times in my life where He has swooped in and saved me from myself and from the enemy's snares. Several times I have even seen the plans of the enemy develop right before my eyes. I am so grateful for God's love and His gift of discernment.

Chapter 1
My Heartache

The peace of the Lord does not come over night. Well, it could if the Lord sees fit. But for me it took years.

I started visiting Temple Aron Hakodesh in 1996, and attended a couple of times a month. I would go for the praise and worship and leave before the message. My friend Marilyn would just look at me and smile, when I gave her a hug and said goodbye. I did not realize then that I was missing out on the messages that the Lord had prepared for me. I just assumed that singing and praising Him was enough. I remember one time I was there standing with my hands up singing and looked up to see a lady with a peaceful, happy smile, dancing as if she had no care in the world. I thought, "Wow, she looks so peaceful. I'll never have that peace."

You see, my life was a roller coaster of drama for as far back as I can remember. Every day there was some sort of chaos. It was that way for my whole circle of family and friends. I remember spending hours on the phone with my sister or a friend crying with each other about one disaster or another. We would not hesitate to call each other even in the middle of the night.

May the God of hope fill you with all joy and peace as you trust in Him, so that you may overflow with hope by the power of the Holy Spirit. **Romans 15:13**

As I started going to service, hearing the songs, and reading of His incredible love for me, my life slowly changed. Again,

Shortly after that he came into the room and said, "Lisa, I need you to come with me." I said, "What about Destiny?" He told me Joan would take care of her because he needed me to come with him. He was silent in the truck, and for some reason I asked no questions. As we drove down Sunrise Boulevard, I remember thinking, "If we go straight on Sunrise Boulevard then he is going to help his friend, but if we go on the Turnpike we are going to my sister, Beverly's house." Well, we got on the Turnpike and the tears just filled my eyes. I had no idea why I was crying. My elderly father lived at my sister's house, along with my sister, her family, and my son Magic. So, I assumed that something happened my dad.

When we arrived at the house the yard was full of teenagers. My husband, whom I simply call G, still had not said a word during entire drive to Hollywood. When I got out of the truck, they all came running up to me. My nephew was in my face shouting, "Aunti, the kids broke in a house and one got shot and they think it was Magic. He's DEAD!" All the muscles in my legs gave way, and I dropped to the ground on my knees! My life would never be the same.

I went in the house to my sister's room and tried to call my sister, because she was at the scene of the crime, and I wanted to go to see for myself. No one would tell me where it was because the police did not want anyone there. I kept trying to dial the phone number, but it wouldn't go through. Every time I dialed, I messed up and had to start over. It dawned on me at that very moment that THIS was my dream from yesterday morning! It was as though God had warned me, tried to prepare me, somehow trying to soften the blow.

The police arrived at my sister's house to inform me that they had my son's body, and he was being transported to the morgue. They were very rough and standoffish to me, the mother who just lost her child. They had absolutely no compassion for my loss. I felt like they thought I was the mastermind in the crime that had just been committed. I asked where the morgue was so I could go see the body. They told me the morgue did not allow people inside. They informed me that I would need to get the funeral parlor to bring the body to the funeral home so I could view it there. I could not understand this procedure they had. How did I know this was my son's body in the morgue, since no family member identified the body? Why should I have to go and obtain funeral home services when I was not even sure this was my child? I was gruffly told, "Yes, it was your son. He has a "Lisa" tattoo on his arm."

With the help of my sister Beverly, we chose Boyd Funeral home. The funeral home could not get the body from the morgue until they were paid a hefty deposit. Imagine if there was a case of mistaken identity and it was not my son laying in that morgue. However, it was my son.

Beverly and I were sitting in the office at the funeral home filling out all the paperwork. The staff member told us that they had body and we would be able to view it soon. I was crying as I said to him, "Doesn't he have the most beautiful face?" When I excused myself to use the restroom, the man said to my sister, "Does she know that they shot him in the face and it is a mess?" "NO, they did not tell her that!" Beverly responded. "She was told he was shot in the chest."

When I came back into the room my sister said, "Lisa, before we go in to view him, you need to know that Magic was shot in the face as well as his chest." I sat there and cried, and then we went in to view his body, and I cried more. His beautiful

15

face was a mess. In fact, the day after the funeral I drove back to the funeral home to speak with the manager. I just had to tell them they did a beautiful job on my son. With only pictures to go by, they transformed the mess back into my beautiful son. You would not know by looking at him in that coffin that he was shot in the face. I appreciated that more than you can imagine.

My son was well liked by many. He was loving and funny to those who knew him well. Yes, he was a gang member who did a lot of unscrupulous things, but many never saw that side. I am not the mother who says, "My child would never do that!" I live in reality. And the reality was my son chose to steal, cheat, drink, do drugs and all that goes with it. The strange part was that he would go to temple on Friday night and then go hang out with trouble on Saturday nights. He just couldn't seem to grasp life as it should be. This is true for far too many young ones in this world today.

He gives power to the weak, And to those who have no might He increases strength. <u>*Isaiah 40:29*</u>

When Magic passed away there were teenagers filling the house daily during the entire week before we buried him. By hugging each child that entered the house, comforting them, and listening to their stories, I obtained the strength to bury my child. Many of them were gang members wearing their black bandanas to show their colors. As they came through the door, I would hug them and take off their black bandannas promising to put them in the coffin and they could take them back after the funeral. There was to be no violence or drama as we said goodbye to our son.

16

Since Magic was a known gang member, the police had several cruisers parked at both ends of the block during the entire week before the funeral. They watched from a distance but did not come close to the house out of respect for the grieving family. I also requested that the police not accompany us from the funeral parlor to the cemetery, since they had accompanied Magic to and from detention center and jail since he was 12 years old, and I added to that fact, that it was a police officer that took his life. They respected my request and stayed away.

The first time I spoke in public was at my son's funeral, and I used his death as a message to the two hundred people (about 70% of the guests were teenagers) who came to the funeral. The blessing at my son's funeral was when more than fifty teenagers got on their knees at his grave side and accepted Jesus in their hearts!

Two days after the funeral I stood on the altar at temple and told the congregation how Awesome our God is. I shared that He brought my boys to temple four years earlier, so they would lead me to temple, that I may learn of His love and form a relationship with Him, so that I would have the strength to say goodbye. I don't know how someone could handle this loss without having the Hem of His garment to hold on tightly.

God had this all planned out to HIS perfection: Magic was supposed to be in jail awaiting trial with his brother and cousin. They broke into a drug dealer's house. Jamie, my youngest son, was the lookout while Magic and Junito, my nephew, went in and stole drugs and liquor. Somehow, they opened the jail cell doors and let Magic go while the other two still sat in jail pending court and eventually served four years

got past the shock, I drove to Suzanne's job to pay her a little visit. I gave her the engagement ring that Magic's father got me along with a gift for the baby and a letter telling her that I will always be there for my first grandchild. Little did I know at the time that Magic would not live past age eighteen. God gave me a piece of Magic. What an Awesome gift!

So Many Questions:

During the time that I was preparing to bury my son and for several months following his death I was on a vengeance. I wrote three letters to the homeowner.

During the day on that fateful Friday, Magic was hanging out at McArthur High School with all his friends. Though he dropped out of school, he would still hang out at the school all the time. That night Magic was at football game drinking and clowning around with his friends.

As the story is told, one of the girls in the group was telling them that she wanted to get some new rims for her car. Magic had the bright idea on how they could get the money for those rims. Four of them made the decision to ride through the neighborhoods and break into some homes. They would sell whatever they got and use the money for those rims.

They had a system: Olga, who was eighteen years old drove the car and kept it running. Jasara who was sixteen years old would knock on the door and if no one answered the boys would break in. Since Kyle was very heavy, Magic would crawl through the window and go through the house to open the door for Kyle.

They broke into three houses that night. You know the saying "Three-Strikes-You're out?" That saying has so much meaning to me now. The first two homes were vacant and there was nothing to steal. They chose their third home. Jasara knocked on the door and waited. No answer. Magic went around the back and broke the window. He thought he heard a noise, so they all ran back to the car and drove off. They rode around the block a few times, but saw no light on in the home, so they went back. As soon as Magic got in the window, they heard gunshots and the other three teenagers took off, leaving their friend behind.

It is sad to say that Kyle was so high when this happened, he went straight home and slept an entire day before he even realized his friend was dead.

When the police arrived, they found Magic lying on the floor in the hallway with a gun in his right hand. Mistake #1: Magic was a lefty.

So, my mind was filled with thoughts. This police officer did not answer the door and he waited in the dark for the intruder to return. He shot him dead the minute he entered the house, then he dragged the body down the hallway to make it look like self-defense. As a police officer he could have made better decisions. He could have turned on the light and let them run away. He could have shot him in the leg or held the gun on him waiting for back up. But, no, he chose to shoot him in cold blood. So, my heart was angry at his decision to end my son's life.

But God held me tight and filled me with knowledge and understanding. He reminded me, that even though this man was a police officer who could have done things differently, first and foremost he was a homeowner who had the right to sleep safely in his own home without any intrusions.

The first two letters to the officer were not mean. They were just full of why's. The third letter was a mother telling the office that I forgive him for his decision he made, and that I was sorry that my son put him in the position where he had to make a decision. He should have been safe in his own home. My son had no business there. That is the most important thing to remember. My son should have been out working a 9-5 and taking care of his daughter. But he made choices that were not biblical or wise.

> **Those who work their land will have abundant food, but those who chase fantasies will have their fill of poverty. Proverbs 28:19**

From the day my son died, I was desperate to reach out to the youth and tell them that this young man went out of this world for nonsense!   You see, he was hanging out, drinking, doing drugs, stealing, and being a nuisance to society. He would not work because the money was not good enough.

I stayed in my room for weeks writing and praying. I created a poster and had more than 4000 printed. I searched the internet for addresses of all the youth facilities and programs in Florida. I sent them out with letters to each one of those addresses along with one for all the judges and representatives in Broward County. Then I went further and sent them to the White House and to all the state senators and representatives whose addresses I could find on the internet. The poster had a photo of Magic alone and another of him holding his baby, with the message, "He died breaking in to a house so he could buy rims for a friend. Was it worth it?"

Let me share with you that the three remaining friends were all charged with Magic's murder. Though they did not pull the trigger, since they were all committing the crime together, they were charged.

Olga, the driver of the getaway car, who was an eighteen at the time, was given probation due to the fact that she was a single mom to a baby girl with no one to care for her, and another fact that it was her first offense. Jasara, the sixteen-year-old girl that knocked on the doors to make sure no one was home, was tried as an adult, found guilty of second-degree murder and burglary. She served three years in prison. Kyle, who was eighteen years old -the one that was so high he went home and slept for hours not comprehending that his friend was dead, was tried as an adult for second degree murder, burglary, and grand theft of a firearm. He served six years in prison.

> ***Blessed be the God and Father of our Lord Jesus Christ, the Father of mercies and God of all comfort, who comforts us in all our affliction so that we will be able to comfort those who are in any affliction with the comfort with which we ourselves are comforted by God.* 2 <u>Corinthians 1:3-4</u>***

I went through many emotions and phases during that time. God gave me wisdom, strength, ideas, and His perfect peace that surpasses all understanding. I do not know how any woman could bury her child if she did not have a real relationship with God to keep her strong.

there was a better life out there. I married him, though we already fought all the time and he cheated on me constantly. I lived with the verbal and physical abuse for more than fifteen years. I would always feel that I was not good enough, not pretty enough, or not smart enough. Every day there was a fight about something. I can look back at every outing or family event and remember what problem occurred that day. He used drugs, he cheated constantly, and many nights he would not even bother to come home. Still, I stayed, praying he would change and that he would love me. I had no real idea of how a marriage should be, since it was just my mother and her girls living together from age seven until she passed.

I was married for two years before my firstborn son whom I call Magic was born. Oh my, who could ever imagine that feeling of holding your very own baby in your arms! He was the light of my life, my curly haired, dimpled baby boy who had blue eyes that changed just before he was a year old. His mystical eyes were so rare that depending on his mood or the light, his eyes would change from green, to gray, to light brown with specs. What an amazing feeling to be a mommy to this beautiful baby boy! He was such a fun and happy baby.

When Magic was a year and a half old, my second son Jamie popped into our world. He was a handful. My Jamie was born with disorders of his brain that they labeled ADHD and later in life diagnosed with Bipolar Disorder. He was always a fussy baby, who never slept at night. There was no time to rest, as he demanded constant attention. From the first encounters at daycare when he would not behave, to this day, he still struggles with the disorder. My heart has always ached for him because he has never known peace.

⁹ Two are better than one, Because they have a good reward for their labor. ¹⁰ For if they fall, one will lift up his companion. But woe to him who is alone when he falls, For he has no one to help him up. <u>Ecclesiastes 4:9-10</u>

Two years after Jamie was born, my best friend, Debbie, became very sick with complications due to Juvenile Diabetes. I opened our home to Debbie and her four-year-old daughter, Alicia. Several months later Debbie was admitted into a nursing facility with hospice. Alicia remained in our home so that she would be close enough to visit her mommy often. The plans were for Alicia to go live with her aunt in another state after Debbie passed away. However, a few months before she passed, Debbie called me and said, "Lisa, I have some bad news, my sister is having difficulties in her family, and she cannot care for Alicia, so I guess you are stuck with her." I responded, "I have wanted to keep her from day one, but did not want to interfere in your plans for her. It will be a blessing to be her second mommy." So, Alicia, who was the same age as Magic, became my daughter, and just as I promised my friend, to this day I still cherish and lover her as much as I could if she were born to me. It was heartbreaking to have to watch my best friend suffer. I would take Alicia to see her every weekend. I would call her up daily, and I would sing to her. I remember crying on the phone and singing, "That's what friends are for." It was hard to lose my best friend. The strength I received, was from the beautiful gift she and the Lord entrusted to me.

So, there I was twenty-four years old, with three toddlers and an abusive husband. Friends, there was plenty of drama! Drama from age seventeen until age forty. Drama with a capital D. Through the first and much of the second marriage, there I was searching the streets looking for my husband all night, chasing him down, fighting, crashing my car into his, stabbing, breaking up, making up, and so much more. My life was full of drama. Drama was all I knew.

Unfortunately, my children grew up in the drama. I tried not to let them see me when I was depressed or sad. However, they witnessed many fights and chaotic scenes while they were growing up. I tried my best to be a good mother and always put them first. However, when I was caught up in the moment, I could never control my need to confront situations immediately. I would wake the kids and buckle them in their car seats at 3 am to search for their daddy.

I remember one time I was dropping Raohl at work. Little Magic, who was about 2 years old, sat in the back in his car seat. When his daddy got out of the car, he opened the back door, reached in and hugged Magic, and said, "I love you." Magic said, "I love you daddy," but as we drove away, my son called his daddy a vulgar name. I was so shocked, I thought that I imagined it. However, the next day he did the same thing. It was then that I had an image of myself using that same vulgarity. Whenever Raohl was not home it would irritate me. I would find myself wondering where he was, who he was with, and why he couldn't be home with his family like normal relationships. When I would walk through the apartment and look at the kitchen door, I would get so irritated that I said that vulgar name to myself, but out loud. I knew my husband couldn't hear me, because he wasn't home. However, my son sure heard.

Needless to say, my children learned drama from us and lived it. I did not learn drama when I was a child. I gained it by dating my first husband at age fifteen and settling on the first person who came into my life. I did not know better. I carried that drama with me through my first marriage and well into my second marriage.

One day, after fifteen years with the husband, I finally had enough. After a heated argument over nothing and his outburst of breaking something shattering glass all over, I was absolutely ready to call it quits. When I dropped him off at work the next morning, I hugged him, said goodbye like all was well, and then I drove straight to the courthouse for a restraining order. He was not allowed to come home.

Three years later I met my second husband, whom I call G. Let me tell you, a man who with deep-rooted issues from his past, who was a self-determined loner, and a woman with severe issues from her past, who had no self-esteem and severe trust issues are not a great match. The poor man got me, with three children and all my emotional baggage. He was not used to drama and he walked right into it! He was not strong enough in his own walk with the Lord to reach out and help me. We suffered through years of arguments and breakups. However, by the Amazing Grace of God we are still together twenty-five years later, living a calm and quiet life.

In 1995, my sons were staying over at their father's house at times. One day, they decided it would be cool to throw rocks at the children in the elementary school behind the apartments. The school was Sar Shalom, a part of Temple Aron Hakodesh. Rabbi Joe (who was the youth pastor at the time) and Marilyn went out to stop their mischief. When Rabbi Joe tells the story, he says that he was getting ready to scold them and at that moment he heard "Show them Love."

am probably calling to share an awesome praise report with her. She is the first person I call whenever the Lord touches my day.

Then we have Rabbi Joe and his wife Ilene. If I need advice on how to handle a situation it is either Rabbi Joe or Rebbetzin Ilene that I will reach out to for sound Godly advice. When I met Rabbi Joe, he was the youth pastor at TAK. Rabbi Joe is the first person who encountered my children as they were throwing rocks at the temple. He was my first phone call when Magic died. They, along with Marilyn, were right by my side when I buried my son.

The funeral had such a powerful effect on the youth, that we organized a weekly Bible study at my sister's home in Hollywood for all of Magic's friends that accepted Jesus at his grave that day. Rabbi Joe, Marilyn and another couple Diane and Nick (from temple) and I, met with these teens every week for more than a year. There was always a house full of teenagers sharing the Word with us. Magic even had some close friends who were not Christian, and they would come every week and talk with us, but they would sit on the porch when it came time to open the Bible and study His Word. They did not come in for the Bible study, but they were there on time on that porch every week. Only God knows what they heard from the open door or window. Only God knows if indeed the seed was planted inside any one of those young teens sitting on that porch.

I started a group that I called Reach4OurTeens. Whenever I participated in youth events Marilyn and Rabbi Joe would be right by my side to reach out to these teens. I love their hearts that are so eager to reach out and tell of Yeshua's love for us. I call Marilyn and Rabbi Joe "My Ride or Die Peeps," which was a phrase the young folks would say in the late 90's. They are the first two calls I would make for anyone who needs prayer or for any praise report.

We went to the Juvenile detention centers and live-in programs to speak. We participated in events and parades. We often involved my family members and the group of Magic's friends in the events. It was such an awesome feeling to hear when one of those teens would give their life to Jesus. This went on for about four years until I got custody of my granddaughter and my priorities switched.

Now, twenty-six years later, I cannot count all the friends He has put in my life who are positive and live for Him. While I write this, I would like to acknowledge the fact that I have been blessed with many family members and good friends in my life before that prayer for believing friends. I don't want to hurt any feelings as I give testimony of the people God has placed in my life.

I will never judge or belittle anyone for the lifestyles they choose, because just a short time ago my life was chaos. I love all my family and friends with a passion. I just feel bad for those who do not have that Perfect Peace in their heart, the Peace that surpasses all understanding. Some are doing well in their day to day lives and others are lost in a world of struggles. I can only pray that they find the peace that I found.

I have also lost family members because of my new life. I guess I am not fun to them anymore or they feel I changed. Some even say, "Oh, Lisa, you're so high and mighty now that you found God." My heart aches that my loved ones feel this way. It is very surreal when someone that has held a special place in your heart for years, that you spoke with often, and was an integral part of your life, suddenly finds themselves so angry with you, but cannot tell you why. You try to do what God says to be reconciled with them, but you end up hitting a brick wall. At least you know you tried but your heart still will grieve for that void in your life. Still, God says "Show them Love."

23 So if you are offering your gift at the altar and there remember that your brother has something against you, 24 leave your gift there before the altar. First go and be reconciled to your brother; then come and offer your gift. **Matthew 5:23-24**

12 Now brother will betray brother to death, and a father his child; and children will rise up against parents and cause them to be put to death. 13 And you will be hated by all for My name's sake. But he who endures to the end shall be saved. **Mark 13:12-13**

You see, I am not perfect and will never pretend to be. There is only One-Who Is Perfect, and He is at the right Hand of our Father. Day to day I pray to be a better person. I have made many wrong choices in my life. The enemy knows how to sneak in with temptations. Even after years of going to temple and being on the dance ministry and prayer ministry I allowed the enemy to grab hold of me, and I stopped attending temple for over a year and a half while I was out doing my thing. I saw the enemy hand me that rope to hang myself with. I took that rope from him and continued swingy wildly holding on for dear life for almost two years.

16 So I say, walk by the Spirit, and you will not gratify the desires of the flesh. 17 For the flesh craves what is contrary to the Spirit, and the Spirit what is contrary to the flesh. They are opposed to each other, so that you do not do what you want. **Galatians 5:*16-17***

However, I am back at temple and have been serving the Lord with a vengeance for the past six years. I will never forget all the times He showed His face while I was out there or the feeling of His strong tug to get back into His Presence and live right. Now, I live for Him. I love all and pray for those who have not found His perfect peace, but I am not perfect, and I will never pretend to be.

I love the life I am living now. I wake up and raise my hand to Heaven giving Him thanks for another day, I go to my dressing room to get ready for work, and then I drop to my knees to ask for His Presence and ask my petitions for my family and friends, and then off to work I go. I look forward to the weekend, so I can go to temple and to church to hear the Word, to worship, to dance, to praise Him, and to bask in His Presence. I ask Him daily what can I, "Little ole Lisa," do for You?

I still am in awe at the number of friends He has placed in my life from temple and church. Just to receive a "Good morning my beautiful neighbor" text is a beautiful gift from Him.

So, what is my message in this chapter? You want a life full of peace, joy, and fellowship? Ask God to place the people He chooses into your life. Then sit back and watch HIS powerful Hand at work.

People are always telling me, "Make him go." They just don't understand the mind of the man I am married to. I realized that I can only change the way I look at things. I can only change me. I can take my life and do positive things to make God happy and not focus on what lacks in our marriage.

Back to the point of this chapter. This is a message for all of the women who feel they cannot live without a man. The ones searching in all the wrong places for a man to call their own. For those who cannot sit alone for long before their mind starts to wonder who their man is talking to or what he is up to.

I was very insecure. I could not figure out why my husband married me if he did not want a normal relationship. I did not realize that normal to some is not normal to others. My husband was raised in a different culture, where the men are used to stopping by a friend's house for a minute on their way home from work, but end up playing dominoes, listening to music, or just chatting for hours. He would leave home at 6 am for work and not come home until after midnight most days. So, while he was out at his spot hanging out for hours at a time, I was home alone.

I thought married life should be about togetherness, having dinner together, going on vacations together, and enjoying each other's company. To him, married life was providing for his wife and family, and to be there in absolute times of need. It was, and to this day, still is a lonely marriage to a great man.

One day it all came to a head. I could not take the loneliness and lack of communication, so I helped him pack his bags and watched as he drove away from our home. I will never forget the sight of him driving away with the domino table that I gave him for his birthday tied up on the back of his truck.

He would still drop by the apartment to check on me. So, I decided to move away so he would not drop by anymore, because this game was getting old, and I wanted to break the ties for good. I moved to a little apartment near my job. My boys were both in Juvenile programs at the time, so, for the first time ever, I was all alone. I was devastated and felt trapped in despair.

The first week there I could not sleep at night, and I was scared at every little sound. I would sit up all night long and play Slingo on the computer. While playing, I would pleasantly chat and run jokes with the other players in the chat room, and the whole-time tears would be streaming down my face.

One night nearing the end of my first week, I was playing Slingo and crying as usual, when I finally shut off the computer and headed towards my bedroom. As I was walking down the hallway, I suddenly dropped to my knees crying hysterically. I was begging Jesus to help me and fill my heart with peace.

And there it was in front of me: The Scale of Justice. One was up and the other was down. I immediately saw that without realizing it, I held my husband as the most important person in my life. God was showing me He is far more important than any person who is or will walk in my life. So, in my mind I took that scale and flipped it to God up and my husband down. I felt Jesus arms around me, and I knew that I was not alone and that I never would be alone. Man, or no man –I would never be alone. I slept like a baby that night. My life changed so much from that experience.

From that day I was never afraid to be in the house alone again, I realized that while I loved my husband, I did not need him desperately and would be ok if he were not in my life. I slept well for the first time ever without that lonely, doomed feeling. Ever since that night I can go sit in a restaurant and eat a meal enjoying my own company. I even go to the movies alone if there is no one interested in a movie I really want to see.

fear not, for I am with you; be not dismayed, for I am your God; I will strengthen you, I will help you, I will uphold you with my righteous right hand. <u>**Isaiah 41:10**</u>

Thou wilt keep him in perfect peace, whose mind is stayed on Thee: BECAUSE HE TRUSTETH IN THEE. Trust ye in the Lord for ever: for in the Lord Jehovah is EVERLASTING STRENGTH
Isaiah 26:3-4

Chapter 4

Losing my Mom

Today I was thinking that I really needed to add a chapter about my mother. My mother was the most beautiful woman you could ever meet. I am not saying it because she was my mom. Nor am I saying she was beautiful in the physical sense. Although she was very beautiful in all the pictures, I have seen of her as a young girl. She was such a genuine loving and caring person to all who knew her.

Her name was Laura. She was an only child for Joe and Peggy, my grandparents. She grew up in the home my grandpa built on the same street as the farmhouse on which he grew up. There were nine or ten homes belonging to my grandpa's siblings that were built around that farmhouse, along with several rows of hen houses on both sides of the streets. To this day I swear when I walk down around that farmhouse, I can hear the hens clucking although they have been gone for forty years.

My grandpa Joe was one of eleven children. There were two sets of twins. Grandpa was a twin though his twin died, and I cannot remember if he died young or just died before I was born, but I never met him. Grandpa Joe was the best! He was always trying to make us laugh. He would tickle us and make faces at us. He is the one who would dance around the house with me on his feet. He would write me silly letters when I moved to Florida. One day I got mail from him and I opened it up to find a note (that I still have in my keepsake box) that said, "I'm Gonna Spank you!" with a smiley face.

Now that I am older, I am sorry that I never really sat down and asked my mother much about her feelings or her life. I have a few letters she wrote her mom, and I read of some of her feelings through those letters. She never complained in those letters. They were always about how work was or what one of us girls did that week, and so forth. I wish I were a little older or wiser so I could have gotten to know that side of her before she passed.

She was always helping everyone. I never heard my mom gossip or quarrel. My sisters would have friends in trouble and mom would let them stay with us for a few days. My best friend's mom was an alcoholic, and I remember my mother driving Francis all around town trying to find her son's dad, so he could take their mentally disabled son, and Francis could go into rehab. That was an ordeal that I will never forget with Francis hanging out the car window screaming vulgar words at everyone we passed. But my mom was a trouper. She genuinely cared about people. She was just kind and loving.

When I was twelve, Mom's dad, my Grandpa T died. My grandmother had taken care of him for the many years of battling Emphysema. It should have been grandma's time to get a little rest. Instead, my mother began suffering from the same disease and shortly after Grandpa passed away, Grandma T came to stay with us for months at a time to help my mom. Once again, I was too young to realize the toll it must have taken on my grandma to watch her husband and only daughter both suffer for years and die of the same disease.

The first memories I have of being afraid of dying I believe started when my grandpa died. I wrote about that fear in another chapter, because that fear grasped me for years until I finally came to terms with the fact that God brought me here

44

for a time and a purpose. He is in control and He does not make mistakes. Once in a while that old fear will start to pop up, and I just lift my hands up and say, "ABBA, You got this, take it away!"

Well, this story is getting a little long for the purpose of this book. I can get carried away talking about my mom. OH, I loved her so. I wanted to give you a clear picture of who she was and how life with her and losing her impacted my life.

For the last four years of my mother's life, she was in and out of the hospital. She had to quit her job. I can remember her crying, because she did not want to use food stamps. Still, she kept her head up and always had a smile on her face. She made sure I had everything I needed. She made my clothes; she took me to school and attended all my after-school events. She made everyone feel special.

I remember getting so angry, because my mother took it upon herself to take care of this cranky old lady, Mrs. Johnson. Mrs. Johnson lived down the street and was always mean to the kids on the block. She moved in to one of the little apartments in the same yard as our house after she became ill. It turned out that she had Emphysema as well. My mother, who could barely breathe herself, would constantly be taking care of Mrs. Johnson. When my mom died, I was angry that Mrs. Johnson was still alive and kicking. I mean, I was really mad. God forgive me now!

Mom's health got so bad she finally had to have the oxygen machine full time. Due to the fact that she was so sick and she had the oxygen machine, we both made the decision not to have the Sweet Sixteen party that I dreamt of for years. I was not embarrassed by the machine, I just felt bad for my mother.

In 1977, my Dad gave his notice at the company where he worked for thirty years. He was going to come live with us in Florida and help take care of my mom. My sisters were already married and living on their own. My dad was to arrive in April. Remember, they had been separated since I was seven years old. Now, after twelve years of separation, they were finally going to be reunited. However, it was not meant to be.

> *But now, thus says the LORD, who created you, O Jacob, And He who formed you, O Israel: "Fear not, for I have redeemed you; I have called you by your name; You are Mine, When you pass through the waters, I will be with you; And through the rivers, they shall not overflow you. When you walk through the fire, you shall not be burned, Nor shall the flame scorch you.* Isaiah 43:1-2

On March 21st I was getting ready for school. My mother had another episode where she could not breathe. We called the ambulance. I will never forget my mom on that stretcher struggling to breathe. My mom looked up at me and said, "I'm dying." I said, "No Mommy, you are not dying they are going to take good care of you." They put her in the ambulance and my grandma went with her. I thought it was just another trip to the hospital, so I drove to school. I cannot remember if my grandma told me to go to school first and then to the hospital or why that decision was made. However, she had been in and out so many times, I just assumed it was another time and I would go visit her after school. But I do know that I never said, "I love you, Mommy," before they put her on that stretcher.

When school let out for the day, I drove to my sister's house to see if she knew mommy was in the hospital. My sister was not home, so I decided to go home before heading to the hospital. When I got home, the house was full of people including my Grandma, my sisters, and their spouses. Mommy was gone!

My world fell apart that day. The one person who was my world was gone, and I had not even told her that I loved her when they put her on that stretcher! I was sixteen years old, and my mother was gone. This was the only person who I could sit for hours with and tell anything to. I had no idea where I was going from there.

This is my "MOM" song. The song I sing often to my mom:

> *I wake up in the morning and I wonder*
> *Why everything's the same as it was*
> *I can't understand, no, I can't understand*
> *How life goes on the way it does*
> *Why does my heart go on beating?*
> *Why do these eyes of mine cry?*
> *Don't they know it's the end of the world?*
> *It ended when you said goodbye.*
>
> *Song: End of the World by Skeeter Davis*

I cried for years. At nearly sixty years old, I still want my mommy. When I had my children, whenever I am sick, when I am at a loss for what to do, I think of her. I even call out to my mother in the middle of the night if I am sick. I have woken my spouse up by calling "Mommy" in my sleep.

Chapter 5

God's Message to Me- My Destiny Story:

When Magic died, his daughter, Destiny, was nineteen months old. Since the first week after she was born, she would sleep at my house almost every weekend. I would pick her up after work on Friday and bring her home on Sunday night. I always looked forward to our time together.

The night that Magic died, Destiny was at my house. Her mother sat talking to me for a while before she left Destiny for the weekend. Suzanne was all excited, because she was getting married to Curtis, who was Magic's best friend. That night I got the call that changed my world.

Shortly after we buried my son, I noticed a big change in Suzanne. She told me that she did not want Destiny to know anything about Magic. She did not want Destiny to know Magic was her daddy, because she wanted Curtis to be Destiny's daddy. In fact, she did not want Destiny to know about Magic at all. I asked her how was she going to explain her grandma and my side of the family? I reminded her that Destiny looked just like her daddy and that everyone who knew Magic would surely talk about him to her when they saw her. Well, that was a big mistake on my part.

Suzanne suddenly fell off the face of the earth. It took a few weeks before I realized she was avoiding me. I called several times and got no answer. I left her messages and I waited. Years ago, I would have hunted her down like a raging bull! I would have searched high and low and knocked on everyone's door until I found her. I would have cursed her out with the terrible language I used when I was mad. It would not have been a very pretty scene if she had pulled this several years before.

However, I did not lose control. My heart was in a different place due to a peace that surpasses all understanding that was given as a gift from my Father to me. I simply lifted the situation and my granddaughter up to God and let Him take control. Yes, there were many times when I broke down and cried, then prayed and then cried more.

Do you know God listens? Do you He know actually talks to us? Sometimes it is a thought in our head and other times it is through someone else.

Many times, while I was in temple singing and praying, I would lift up my hands and talk to Him in all sincerity. I would say, "ABBA, if you let Destiny back in my life, I will bring her here to temple with me again."

A memory just came to mind: Against company policy, I became very friendly with a resident named Ina. We spoke often on the phone in the year she was waiting to be assigned an apartment. I would go visit her regularly and we would chat. She was from Jamaica and we had many good conversations. It turned out that she received custody of her granddaughter and raised her several years before. When we would discuss Destiny, she would always say, "You are going to raise that girl. She is going to live with you," I would tell her that I did not think that would ever happen and that all I wanted was to be a part of her life. Ina would insist, "I'm telling you that you are going to have that girl full time!"

I never stopped trying to locate Suzanne. I asked around, but no one seemed to have heard from her or Curtis. I researched all the information I could find on Grandparent's rights. I got the name of a lawyer that I was considering calling, but I had no idea where Suzanne and Destiny were.

I will never forget the day (after a year and a half of praying), Rabbi Yosef walked up to the microphone in the middle of worship and said, "I believe I have a message for someone who is desperately seeking a child; If you have it in your heart that you want a child please come to the altar and let us pray for you."

I can still picture the altar and remember being surprised to see a couple of women I was friendly with up there praying for a baby. I had no idea that they wanted a baby at this time in their life. So, I lifted my hands to pray for them and all for all the other women up at the altar.

Sometimes, I have a sense of humor when I pray. When I first married my second husband, I wanted to have a baby with him. I tried but could not conceive. However, when Magic died, that desire for a baby died right along with my son. When I had my hands up in the air praying for these women, my mind jumped to a baby, and I laughed and said, "ABBA, don't let me go there, I don't want a baby, all I want is Destiny!" And I continued to pray for the women at the altar.

That night my father called me and said, "I have a phone number for Suzanne." I was shocked. I wrote the number down and continued working on the computer. The thought came to mind, "Call the number." I told the thought, "No, she won't talk to me I will wait for the lawyer." A second time

52

the thought came, "Call the number." "No, she won't talk to me." Then the third time the thought, "Call the number" came, so I picked up the phone and dialed the number.

Suzanne answered, "Hello."

"Hi Suzanne, how are you and Destiny doing?" I inquired.

Suzanne realizing it was me responded with a puffed-up attitude in her voice, "We are just fine!"

A thought entered my mind, "No attitude Lisa, show her love."

"Oh, that's good." I responded. "I just got your number and am simply calling to say hello and let you know I am always here for you."

"We are doing just great!" Suzanne reiterated.

"That's nice to hear." I continued. "I am not calling to aggravate you. I just want you to know I love you both, and I am here if you ever need me. I miss Destiny very much."

A gentle answer turns away wrath, but a harsh word stirs up anger. Proverbs 15:1

From that point she let her guard down and we started talking. She did not say a lot, but she promised to call me again. She did call me a couple of days later, and I invited her to eat. I told her she did not need to bring Destiny, but she could meet me and we could talk. She agreed. Imagine my surprise when she brought my Destiny into the restaurant with her! I was overjoyed to see my granddaughter's bright smile after a year and a half.

It turned out that Suzanne did not comply and they took her parental rights away. I adopted Destiny. With that adoption she got her last name back and a full scholarship to any Florida university. Destiny had a forever home with her Nona (as she lovingly nicknamed me as a teenager) and Grandpa G. She was a blessing from God, and we cherish that blessing and have done our best to raise her.

Jehovah Jireh – The Lord Will Provide

> *"And Abraham called the name of that place Jehovahjireh: as it is said to this day, In the mount of the LORD it shall be seen." Genesis 22:14*

I had no help when I was raising my three children. Their father was no help and he made sure I took them everywhere I went. My sisters each had their own children, and my boys were both a handful, so I rarely had a moment to myself. However, when God placed Destiny in our home, He placed an army of earthly angels to guard over her. When she was six years old, I signed her up for cheerleading. When I was waiting in the long line to register her, I met a lady named "Sha'Lynne" (AKA Lynne), who was registering her two daughters. We talked the entire time and became very friendly. We also talked the whole time during cheerleading practices. I told her that Destiny was going to miss practice for ten days, because I was having surgery. Lynne stopped at our house every afternoon to pick up Destiny for practice. I was overwhelmed at the offer and her generosity.

It did not stop there. I never went anywhere without my children when they were young. However, when Destiny came to live with us, I traveled for work four times a year. My husband, G, worked late, so he could not pick her up from school. Lynne offered once again to step in. Her home was one of the very few places I would trust for Destiny to sleepover. It was just Lynne and the two girls living at the house, so I knew Destiny was in a safe place. Destiny would sleep over the entire duration and Lynne would transport her to and from school every day, even though Destiny did not go to the same school the girls did. Whenever Lynne planned birthday parties or sleepovers, Destiny was always on the list. She always says, "Destiny is my third daughter." To this day Lynne and I are very close, and I try my best to be there whenever Lynne needs a favor or an ear to listen. You see, I trusted God with the whole situation, and He brought Destiny to a safe home and gave me a village to help raise her.

Yes, I continued to bring her to temple every week. I enrolled her in the temple school. When Sar Shalom school closed its doors, I prayed for financial favor and had the faith to enroll her in Abundant Life Christian Academy, where through another miracle from God, she was accepted with her both morning care and aftercare paid for by an anonymous donor, and she continued her schooling there. G and his daughter Patrice are the ones that God put in Destiny's path to assist with her education. She always turned to them for advice on how to solve a problem, and they continue to advise her with her educational questions. Destiny received a full scholarship to any Florida university and is currently getting ready to graduate college and move on to graduate school to study law.

Now remember, the Rabbi did not say he had a message for someone seeking a baby. No, he said he had a message for someone desperately seeking a child! Yes, God heard my cries! God saw that I was faithful, and He actually spoke to me through that message saying, "Relax my child, you will have that child you so desperately seek."

So, the message from this story is clear. Do not do things the way you would in your former days. Do not storm over to your circumstance and demand control. Give the control to God and trust in Him to handle it for you. He is listening and watching how you respond. He will bless your faithfulness.

Do not be conformed to this world, but be transformed by the renewal of your mind, that by testing you may discern what is the will of God, what is good and acceptable and perfect. **Romans 12:2**

He is before all things, and in Him all things hold together. **Colossians 1:17**

Be watchful, stand firm in the faith, act like men, be strong. **1 Corinthians 16:13**

Chapter 6

My Light in the Darkness

Since I was a little girl, I was always afraid to be alone. I was so afraid to go into the house if it was getting to be dusk and no one was home. When I moved to Florida my mother worked and my sisters were always out and about as most teens are. If I came home from school or from playing and it was still light outside, I was fine to go in the house. If I came home and it was getting dark out, I would ride my bike around the block until someone came home.

I guess somehow, my mother and sisters did not realize that is what I did, now that I think about it. It seems they would have done something to disperse those fears back then, but I do not remember ever talking about the fears to anyone. No, I would just ride around the block, and around the block, and around the block for as long as it took for someone to come home.

Even when I was older the fears continued. I would go in the house and look in every closet and under every bed to make sure it was all clear before I could relax. This continued until I was in my late thirties. When my children were little, I would tell them, look under the bed for mommy, and they would look under the bed and say, "Nope, no one there!" I knew then it was not a natural reaction to the fear. But now as I write, I wonder why my mother or family never noticed this behavior or discussed these fears with me.

One day while I was in counseling, the therapist said, "Something tragic must have happened when you were a child." I told her that I did not remember anything tragic, and

Chapter 7

Miracles - Prayers on Our Knees

In March of 2019 I was at temple. While I was standing there with my arms up singing and worshipping, I looked over at my friend Marilyn. A memory of Marilyn and Destiny as a toddler both on their knees popped in to my head. I remembered how Marilyn used to always be on her knees praying by her seat.

When Destiny was a toddler, she would get on her knees beside Marilyn. I thought it was cute that Destiny was mimicking Marilyn. However, after a couple of weeks I realized that she was not just mimicking Marilyn. She was indeed praying. It amazed me, that at her young age, this prayer was serious business to her. She was on her knees praying and having her own conversations with the Lord.

Upon remembering this I turned to Marilyn and said, "When's the last time you prayed on your knees?" Marilyn looked at me and said, "WOW." At that time, I just figured that it was a message from God to Marilyn, because she had somehow gotten out of this practice. Maybe it was because we were twenty years older so getting down there was a little more difficult.

However, that entire week I kept getting the nudge that I should be on my knees. I realized then that this message was not just for Marilyn, it was for me too! God wants us all on our knees. I never had the practice to get on my knees to pray. Though I prayed often it was never on my knees.

I had been using Destiny's room as my dressing room since she went away to college. This way I could put my make up on and get dressed every morning without waking my husband. So, with this persisting feeling, I decided I was going to pray on my knees before leaving that room in the morning.

Praying on my knees has become my way of saying, "Lord, I love You and I take this talk with You and our time together very serious." Funny, when I first started getting on my knees I would only do it on the week days before I went to work. Then one morning about a month later it dawned on me, "Why am I not doing it on the weekends?" I immediately started praying every day on my knees before I went downstairs.

Within a few weeks of me going to my knees in prayer, I witnessed another miracle of immediate answer to prayer: My granddaughter, whom I called Princess LeeLee, was taken away from her mother right after her birth. Isis, her mother, was a drug addict who was high through her entire pregnancy. In fact, she was high while giving birth to her daughter. My son James is her father, and he was in prison again, serving four years this time.

LeeLee was less than a week old when the judge asked if I would be willing to keep her. Though it broke my heart, I had to face the fact that I could not raise another child. I was still meeting the needs of my granddaughter Destiny, whom I adopted eleven years earlier. Destiny still had to get through three more years of college. I also knew that at the age of fifty-six it was not fair to LeeLee for me to take her. LeeLee deserved to have a mommy who would keep up with her for the next twenty years. Someone who would have the energy to ride all the park rides and drive her to all her practices for school activities.

Quickly, I thought of a plan B. My daughter Alicia was raising her two daughters in Ocala (about five hours away from me). She had just gotten an apartment through the housing authority for herself and her daughters. Alicia wanted to give LeeLee a home, and I thought that LeeLee would be safe with Alicia and her girls.

It took four months to get Alicia approved with the courts. Isis and James had agreed to terminate their rights so that Alicia could go through with the adoption. I purchased all her furniture, toys, clothing, diapers, and food to get her started, and I promised to provide financially for her. I packed LeeLee up and drove her to her new home that Thanksgiving weekend.

All seemed to be going well for over a year. We talked often, and Alicia and the three girls came to visit a couple of times during that year. I even drove up and spent a few days with them to celebrate LeeLee's birthday. That is when I realized, that Alicia had the girl's father living with them. She assured me that Child Net knew he was there and that all was on the up and up.

Then one day I got a call from Alicia telling me that that she lost her apartment, and she, her boyfriend and the three girls were temporarily staying with her boyfriend's mother in a two-bedroom apartment along with two other adults. I told her that she needed to call ChildNet right away, as the adoption was not yet final and their rules are that they know where the child is at all times. The following Monday, Child Protective Services came and took LeeLee away.

The case worker would not tell me why they took LeeLee away so fast without giving Alicia the opportunity to cure whatever needed to be cured. Alicia assures me that me she has not clue as to why LeeLee was taken. However, ChildNet usually gives the adult opportunity to cure and enrolls them in classes. That is, unless something is severe and they feel the child is in danger. Therefore, ChildNet must have had a substantial evidence to remove her from the home. They wouldn't discuss the case with me at all. I was told that since James terminated his parental rights that my grandparent rights were also terminated. They could not tell me where the baby was nor could they reveal the plans they had for her.

I was heartbroken. This was my granddaughter. For some reason, when she was born and I held her for the first time, I felt my mother. From that moment on there was a special bond in my heart that I cannot really describe with words. I have never felt my mother in my children or any of my grandchildren. I trusted still, knowing that our God is great and He had LeeLee in the palms of His Mighty Hands. I knew that He was protecting her from something that I was unaware of in her life.

There was a couple who had been her foster mothers for the first four months of her life. They had her again and said they were willing to adopt. For some reason they decided not to adopt and from that point I had no idea where LeeLee was. I cried a lot and I prayed even more. I wrote letters to the judge. I also wrote a long letter for them to give to the adoptive parents. I wanted them to know that my life was drama free and that I would not cause any hindrance in their lives. I

show I am thinking of them. One day I sent a care package just to brighten their day. It had clothes and toys for the children and a gift card for the parents whose income has been cut.

On the week of LeeLee's 4th birthday, I created a Drive-By party, surprising even the parents. Of course, I asked permission from the parents to drop balloons and a card off on their porch for them to give LeeLee. However, they were surprised that I made a huge party out of it. I had spent a few weeks gathering outfits for both the children. I have always had this practice to treat all the children in one home the same. I would never want her brother to feel unloved. They each got bag of clothes with balloons hanging from them, along with an ice cream cake, flowers and a card for Mom and Dad to remind them how special they are to me, and lunch from McDonalds for them all. One perfectly planned Drive-By party.

> *Oh come, let us worship and bow down; let us kneel before the LORD, our Maker! Psalm 95:6*

I thank the Lord because HE blessed my efforts. I did not expect to see the children because of the COVID-19 quarantine. I had planned to drop everything at their door and drive away. Before I arrived, I got a message from LeeLee's mommy saying text me when you get here. So, I put everything at their door and texted her to tell her I was there. Imagine my surprise when they brought LeeLee and her brother out in the yard to wave and talk to Nona! My heart melted when LeeLee said, "So, how is work, Nona?"

My message in this long story is how quickly God answered those prayers from my heart on my knees. Also, how the prayers at the beginning were selfish and went unanswered. The minute my heart turned to His perfect will and her well-being. God blessed my prayers.

for it is written, "As I live, says the Lord, every knee shall bow to me, and every tongue shall confess[a] to God." Romans 14:11

Your knees can take you where your feet cannot.

Chapter 8

Purple Roses

Note: for this story I changed her name out of respect.

In August of 2017, we had the TAK Women's Retreat, which was a two-night and three-day event held at the Ritz Carlton Hotel in Naples, Florida. While I felt His Presence at the previous retreats, this retreat was so powerful and anointed that I will never forget the experience.

You could feel His Presence the moment you entered the conference room. The message was given by Rebbetzin Jamie Lash and was all about God and the heart. The colorful flags for worshipping were lined up around the entire room. My eyes fell on a side table that had dozens of the most beautiful purple roses. My heart leaped at the sight of these roses.

During the weekend we would break out into groups and pray. Each time I was in a group, the prayer was so powerful and kept focusing on restoration of families, forgiveness, and His perfect peace in our lives. I cannot describe the feeling in the room for those three days which was the Overwhelming Presence of Adonai.

Saturday morning as Rebbetzin Jamie was speaking, once again my eyes fell on the roses. The thought came to mind, "You need to bring one of those roses to Emiline." That stopped me in my tracks, and I laughed while speaking to my thoughts, "Wow, where did that come from? You know that lady doesn't want anything from me."

Let me take a step back just to say, Emiline is the one person I know of who cannot stand me. She hates me with a passion. She is the mother of my husband's children. His children lived in our home with us since they were fifteen years old, they completed high school, one of them four years of college, and they even had babies while staying in our home before stepping out on their own. I enjoyed them living in our home and tried my best never to scold or to try to parent them as I knew they had a mom and a dad.

Emiline arrived in the US in 2012. In fact, on the day of her arrival, she was invited into our home for dinner. The family had a delicious meal and enjoyed the evening chatting. I was happy that the girls had their mother close to them at last, and I thought she and I would be friends. We had spoken on the phone a few times over the years, and she was always pleasant. However, for some reason she has chosen to not like me. I believe she may have had other expectations where my husband was concerned. I leave that matter for them and God to handle.

Ever since my husband became a part of my life, I have always and will continue to include Emiline in my prayers. When I pray for family, her name comes out of my mouth right along with her children and our grandchildren. When she first came to Florida, she shared an apartment with her eldest daughter. Since she feels so strongly against me, my husband's daughters, who shared our home for many years, have chosen not to come to our house nor to invite me to any of the family events. They are not rude to me when they see me, I am just excluded from that part of my husband's life. So, for several years since Emiline's arrival, the holidays were lonely and hard to endure.

I kept asking God what did it mean with the roses, "One alone won't survive but two together will survive?" I know in my heart He meant that Emiline and I should live good together. Ever since I started dating my husband and I learned of his family back home, I always felt something in my heart for Emiline. It is very weird, but I always felt a heart connection. I am sure she does not feel it. I never want to see any woman hurt. I did not break up a happy home, but I am pretty sure she thinks I did. I believe if we were friends, which would be possible if there were nothing to hide or if there were no jealousy, then all our lives would be complete, because the entire family could share both the joys and the sorrows of life together.

I got home just before 6 pm. When I got home, G was sitting at the counter watching television. I walked in with the roses and I said, "G, would you please give these to Emiline?" He looked at me like I had two heads. I was still shaking, and I continued to tell him the story of the retreat and the roses.

All of a sudden, I started crying and I blurted out, "You see, because she hates me, I have been excluded from a huge part of your life; because she hates me, I cannot visit my mother-in-law who lives with her; because she hates me, I cannot enjoy holidays and family gatherings with you and the children. Our marriage is miserable because of this division. I don't hate her; she just can't stand me. If you give her these flowers and tell her of the message that I got from God, maybe she will know it came from God and it will bring her peace, and she maybe she will reconsider and open up her heart so we could all share life together."

I told him that he was the only one that could break this division. He could stand in the gap and bring the two of us together to reconcile the differences, so we could all be a peaceful blended family.

I left the roses on the counter. G closed his eyes and rested his head where he sat for a while. Then much to my dismay, he left the room and went upstairs to sleep. I just sat there stunned for quite a while.

I called Marilyn crying, "I did exactly what I thought God wanted me to do!" Marilyn quickly spoke: "Those roses were not supposed to get to Emiline! They were for G! You opened up your heart and told him everything that you have had bottled up for years. Those roses were for G!"

Even as I write this, I ponder the reasoning behind these roses. I mean, look at the message that is as bold as can be, **"Because one alone won't survive, together the two will survive."** I believe God is telling me, what I have always felt in my heart also, the fact that she and I share a bond. She has been in his life since they were teenagers, and he has an obligation in his heart to her, so they will always be family. If something were to ever happen where my husband was bedridden or in the hospital, I would not want it to be awkward for us.

That is just the way my heart ticks. Most people would think I was crazy for thinking like this, but I cannot ignore the tug in my heart for her. In fact, a few weeks ago during a message in service, I started wondering what is stopping us from having a friendly relationship. Suddenly I realized that God gives us our friends, so if we are not friends even after all of my efforts of becoming friends, then we were not meant to be friends.

Still, I hold out the olive branch. Still, I vow to show her love.

Yet even now, says the LORD, return to me with all your heart, with fasting, with weeping, and with mourning; rend your hearts and not your clothing. Return to the LORD, your God, for he is gracious and merciful, slow to anger, and abounding in steadfast love, and relents from punishing. **Joel 2: 12-13**

Chapter 9

He Spared Me

Below are examples of how God covered me and spared me from watching my loved ones take their final breaths.

My Grandma's passing: When my grandmother passed away, I would have been the one to find her.

When my grandmother broke her hip in the late 80's, I moved into her home with my children, so she would not be alone. Then we all moved to Florida where my Grandma lived with us for a few more years.   I began working nights and her Alzheimer's got worse, so Grandma moved in with my sister Beverly and her family, where she spent her final years.

My grandmother had late-stage Alzheimer's and did not really know who we were most days near the end of her life.   Every time I went to my sister's house, I would spend time talking to Grandma about silly things, even if she did not know what I was talking about. I would tell her this handsome guy named Joseph wanted to meet her and she would say, "Oh, Noooo."

I will never understand this disease that will wipe away the memories of the "love of your life" or your only child. Sometimes she remembered her teen years but her husband and daughter were no longer there. However, anytime I visited my sister's home I would go straight into my grandma's room to give her a hug before talking to anyone else.

I can't recall if it was the day Magic died or the following day, I was at my sister's house, which was full of family and friends, I would often feel overwhelmed and leave the house to go walking alone. This time as I was walking and crying, I heard Magic say, "Mommy, where were you? I was calling you." It was loud and clear in my ears. That haunted me for some time that he was calling me and I could not help him.

I realize that God once again spared me from watching a loved one die. Though Magic's death was horrible, I am sure that Jesus held His arms out to Magic and carried him home. But as a mother, not being able to stop that fatal blow, it is not easy to get over that feeling of failure. I could not stop him from his behavior, and I could not stop the inevitable from happening. However, my God gave me His perfect peace when I finally laid it in His Hands. I see how God spared me from seeing the bullets pierce my son's face and chest or watching as he dropped to the ground struggling for his final breath. He gave me peace in knowing that HE loves me and protects me.

For several months I would say, "God, please let my son be in Heaven. I know he did wrong, but please let my son be in Heaven." I even had a couple of dreams where I was with Magic, and I asked him if he was in Heaven. One day it finally dawned on me that I had bothered God for too long with this prayer, since it was already said and done. So, I changed the prayer and said, "God, it is finished and whatever the ending was is beyond my control, I am sorry for nagging You and I trust in YOU." That was the last time the thoughts of Magic's final breath tormented me.

My Father's passing: God spared me again when my father passed away. Coincidentally, he was in the same room as my grandma. My father moved in with my sister shortly after my grandma passed away. My father was going to the VA clinic every month. I assumed it was to keep his heart healthy after his triple bypass. However, in 2002, he took sick and we found out that not only did he have cancer, he had stage 4 cancer that had spread. My sisters and I had no idea he even had cancer.

My father and my husband G always had a great relationship. G would visit him and sit on the porch talking for hours. When I went home and told my husband, "Daddy has cancer," my husband replied, "I know, he told me last year." I was a little perplexed that my husband kept it from me but soon realized he was a man of honor and respect. I was glad my father had my husband to confide in.

When my sisters and I found out he was sick, he was already nearing his final days. In fact, he only lived another month. Hospice was set up to take care of him, so he could die in his home instead of the hospital. He was very brave. He refused the pain medication right up to the very end. In fact, the when he finally said he would take some morphine, they did not even get it to the house before he passed.

During the last day of his life my sisters and I, along with most of his grandchildren, were at the house. I remember talking to my dad, who hardly had energy to talk.

"I love you, Dad," I told him.

"I know you do," he responded.

The hospice nurse was there all day. It was 1:30 in the morning and I thought that he would be leaving this world at any moment. However, the hospice nurse told me I should go home and sleep, because it could even be another day or two. When I left his room, I asked him if he needed anything. "Yes, I need a priest," was his response.

My father had only been to church a couple of times in the previous forty years, and he wanted a priest. Marilyn and Rabbi Joe had visited him several times and prayed with him. However, for my dad, this was not enough. He wanted a priest.

I went home to try and get some sleep. At 6 am I gave up on trying to sleep and could not relax, so I decided I would try my best to get my dad a priest. I did not go to a Catholic church, so I did not think this was possible. However, I pulled out the phone book and left messages at several churches in the area. Within fifteen minutes I got a call back from a priest.

"My dad is dying," I explained. "He hasn't been to church in years. He may have an hour or he may have a day but all he wants is a priest."

"I'm on my way," the priest replied.

I left my house in Fort Lauderdale and headed for the twenty-minute ride to my dad's house. I was almost there, when I got a call from my sister who told me that I could take my time, because dad was gone.

I was crushed! I was crying on the phone as I told my sister that I felt horrible, because the one thing my dad ever asked me for was the priest, and I couldn't honor that request. My sister said, "Don't cry Lisa, Daddy got his priest, in fact, the priest did not even get to say a word to Daddy, because the minute he walked into the room Daddy looked up at the priest, smiled, and passed away!"

I am grateful to God that the priest made it to my father just in time to let him go peacefully. And I am positive again, that God spared me from seeing my father's last breath.

My Sister Beverly: My sister Beverly was more than a sister to me growing up. I was blessed with two sisters, Beverly and Joanne. They were there for me when I was young and when I was raising my children alone. I could always call either of them and they would come running.

Since I was just sixteen when my mother died, Beverly became my mother, my sister, and my best friend. We were so close. We went everywhere together. When we were not together, we were on the phone, laughing and chatting for hours. Our families were always together for every holiday. I would go to her house, lay on the bed watching TV, and we would talk for hours. There was a comfort being with her no matter what I was going through.

When she was in her mid-forties, it seems that she let life (or should I say the enemy) get the best of her. She went from being the fun, loving, caring, dependable woman everyone looked up to, to a woman no one recognized. She started dating a man who was in prison when she met him, in fact, he was in and out of prison all his life. He became her world. She did whatever he asked. She got involved in all of his drug dealings. There was always a house full of strangers when I

we had another day with her, I needed to be strong. I left Joey with his mom at 1:30 in the morning and headed home to get some sleep. Shortly after I left JoJo fell asleep. When he woke up twenty minutes later his mom was gone.

It seemed as though she was waiting for us all to be away, so we would not see her last breath. God, once again, spared me from witnessing the passing of my loved one.

Have mercy on me, my God, have mercy on me, for in you I take refuge. I will take refuge in the shadow of your wings until the disaster has passed. Psalm 57:1

Chapter 10

Israel -Trip of a Lifetime

"Ask, and it will be given to you; seek, and you will find; knock, and it will be opened to you for everyone who asks receives, and he who seeks finds, and to Him who knocks it will be opened. <u>Mathew 7:7-8</u>

I thought this book was finished and this morning I awoke with the thought that I did not write about my trip to Israel. I answered that thought: "No, I don't need to tell them about Israel this time." Then I remembered how my Israel trip came about, and I said, "Yes Lord, I do need to tell them about my trip and Your goodness."

Temple hosts a trip to Israel every two years. I never had the desire that many people have to visit Israel. I always thought that it was going to be way too hot for me there. However, in 2015, when the members of temple came back from their trip and were telling all the great stories of their experience, I felt a stirring in my heart. I remember telling Rabbi Joe, "Wow, it sounds great, but I could never go there, because I don't take to heat and sun very well." Rabbi Joe said, "It can get pretty cold there in the end of November."

In 2017, Rebbetzin Ilene was giving the announcements. She began talking about the experiences of the previous Israel trip and announced an upcoming trip for November. When they were almost finished describing the details, she said, "If you want to go and you don't have the money, ask God for the money and if He wants you to go, He will give you the money." So, I closed my eyes and said, "God, if you give me the money I will go."

Three days later a check for $4000 came in the mail. The check was money that I was expecting already to pay off some other debt. Immediately I thought, "Wow, God wants me to go," but then I thought "No God, You don't want me to go. We had a plan for this money already, the devil is just playing with my head." So, I paid what I was supposed to pay with that money and forgot about the trip.

Several weeks later during the announcements Rebbetzin Ilene said once again, "Ask Him and if He wants you to go. He will give you the money." So jokingly I said, "God, if you want me to go you will give me $3000.00." I reminded Him that I did not fall for the enemy's trick the last time. By the time we left temple, I had already forgotten my little jest in prayer.

The following Tuesday I went to approach my boss with a request form to submit to HR department, so I could withdraw money out of my IRA to use for Destiny's housing and book fees. I looked up in the IRA guidelines and saw that while I could not take money out of my account until I was 59 ½ years old, I could take money for her educational fees. So, I prepared a request and brought it in to my boss.

Coincidence? Jim, my boss, had just returned that morning from taking a trip to Israel. When I brought the letter in to his office, he excitedly told me all about his trip, the people he met, the places he visited, and all about his experience. He said, "You really need to go to Israel at least once in your life time!" I told him about temple and the Israel trips they sponsor every other year and the fact that they had one scheduled in a few months. He stated that I should go, and I told him that even though I really wanted to go, I did not see the financial possibility for a trip in the near future.

He said that I should take it out of my IRA, but I shared with him that I was not old enough to take money out for personal use for another two years. "Lisa, you are taking out your money for Destiny's school fees so add the $3000 to the amount to your request letter and go this year," he suggested.

I did just that, my request was approved, and I went to Israel with the group. Yes, God gave me the money to go. However, it was not borrowed money. It was my money from years of hard work. He made a way that I could use a little of my own money to enjoy this opportunity, and He chose the perfect time for me to take the trip.

My visit to Israel was indeed the trip of a lifetime. And while I would love the opportunity to go again, I don't think it could ever compare to this trip. Usually, the group taking the trip is twenty or thirty people. However, this time there only fourteen of us sharing the beautiful experience together. The trip was intimate and exciting. Hillel was our 71-year-old tour guide. He was also an Antiquities Dealer and a Jeweler. That man walked so fast you could hardly keep up with him. He really knew his stuff. He went above and beyond his job description. He even took us to his home to show us his collection of rare finds and gave the Rabbi a gift to bring home.

Israel Experiences: I was blessed to observe the youngest girls in our group, Victoria and Sofia, who were both under fifteen. I watched as these girls followed Hillel around and

but a frequent visitor that seemed nice. I agreed to room with a stranger.

The Saturday before the trip someone came up to me and said, "Jacqueline is here come meet her." I walked over to say hello to Jacqueline and the minute I saw her smile, the tears suddenly came pouring down my face, and I had this warm feeling inside that I cannot describe. I knew without a doubt God had chosen well. She felt it too. We both hugged and talked for a minute.

On this trip Jacqueline and I formed a beautiful bond. Like Hillel and Diana, Jacqueline was 71 years old. She spent forty plus years in Jamaica with her Jamaican husband. We soon learned that that we had something in common. The personalities she described in her husband were so similar to my husband. A lot of things that I hold in my heart she had already experienced. There was no man bashing (as my husband loves to say) when we shared our life stories with each other. She had nothing but love as we spoke. Often during our days when we were talking or when we saw something concerning as we walked, the two of us would stop and pray together. I felt God brought us together to strengthen and comfort each other.

Funny thing about Jacqueline, and I hope she doesn't mind me writing this: She snores! I mean really loud. I thought when I was going away for fifteen days that I would have fifteen days of quiet sleep without hearing snoring (my hubby snores). But instead, not only did I get the snoring, I also got to hear the discussions she was having in her sleep! She was dreaming a lot and moaning. With her permission the following night I recorded her so she could hear. Some people might be upset that they had a snorer as a roommate. But I said, "God, you chose well, help me overlook the snoring and let me sleep well." When she was restless and tormented in her sleep, I was in the next bed praying for the Lord to hold her tight and have His way with her!

Jacqueline and I were like two peas in a pod. Though she was fourteen older than me, we got along so well. I have many pictures of us smiling and enjoying the experience. The one I love is her standing on a chair looking over the wall to see the men's side of the Western Wall. After the trip was over Jacqueline and I remained friends. Though she sold her house and moved several miles away, we still communicate often. I love when we speak on the phone, because her voice is so loving and cheerful. I thank God for pairing us up. He makes no mistakes.

The whole experience was beautiful. What an honor to sit where Jesus may have sat and to get on that little boat and ride out on the Sea of Galilee. That boat ride and the feel of the cold breeze and the rough waves forever stays in my heart. Just the feeling that He was right there! I reached my hand deep inside the roped off areas that we were told Jesus walked and took a few small stones home that could have been touched by Him.

I have a photo of a cloud that looked just like Jesus was hovering above us holding a heart in His Hands. It was as if He was there looking over us. And Rainbows: There were so many beautiful rainbows during our trip. One day while riding in the bus, there was a double rainbow that seemed to follow us for almost an hour. I knew that God was boldly reminding us that He was with us. I could go on and on with the different experiences there.

I am so grateful for the opportunity to go at that appointed time with that group of people. I would love to go again but I realize that nothing will ever top this trip. This gift from God, was truly the "Trip of a Lifetime."

The message in my long story is- Ask Him, and trust that if He thinks it is good for you, He will give it to you.

Chapter 11

His Intricate Blessing

I am almost ashamed to write this portion because I have no business being in a financial bind. The reason I am in a bind is because for years and years I have lived above my means by using credit cards. Yes, my payments for everything have always been early or on time. However, I used my entire paycheck to pay bills, so there was no money left to pull out of my purse. I even went through a debt consolidation and cleaned up my credit once. I should have learned from that, but I got sucked right back in to living above my means, and in no time at all my debt tripled.

Everywhere I went, I pulled out the card. I went to the doctor and pulled out the card, Destiny's school fee came up, I pulled out the card. Each time James came out of prison, he needed everything to start over, so I pulled out the card. Every time I went on a trip with work or for pleasure, I pulled out the card. Needless to say, I was drowning in debt and the interest was choking me.

My husband on the other hand never uses a credit card, lives within his means, and always seems to be able to reach in his pocket to help someone. While I did a lot for others throughout my life, it was always with a credit card in hand.

Since I was a child, I have been a giver. If I saw something that reminded me of someone, I would buy it for them just to make them smile. I remember once I had a friend who loved brass knickknacks, so every time I visited her, I would bring her a new one. Her brother told me one day, "Lisa, stop

This meant paying the lawyer all over again, but at least in five years I would be able to start saving to retire. The lawyer figured out a payment plan, which would be paid in 60 months. He told me that at the end of the hearing process the payment could be lower than quoted.

I prayed to God regarding these circumstances, and I said, "ABBA, please let me make these payments and if You choose to lower the payments a little, then I will continue to make the original payment that was quoted at beginning in order to pay it off sooner."

One Saturday, about a month later, I was assisting in the Altar Prayer ministry. A beautiful young lady with a baby came up for prayer. She had been moving from place to place for ten months with nowhere to call her own. After we prayed and she walked away, I became overwhelmed with thankfulness and awe that the Lord has protected me from so many things. I lifted my hands and said, "ABBA, why? Why have you protected me so much? Why have you blessed me so much? I have never been homeless, jobless, foodless! You ABBA, are so beautiful to me, and I give you my thanks."

That Sunday evening, I went to PenTab church for an outside evening service. I drove there by myself. While I was driving there, I was wondering why I felt this strong urge to go. Suddenly, I said, "Lord, I don't know why I have this urge to go, but I ask that this evening be a blessing to You."

It was such a beautiful experience to be out in the night with the warm breeze, to look up at the moon and the stars with my hands lifted high in praise. During the service three young men came from across the street and they were getting prayed for. Not judging, but you could tell their lives were not going well so far. So, as the church members were praying, I kept getting drawn closer and closer as I was also praying for them. Soon I was right up-front praying whatever the Lord placed in my heart to pray for them. I even felt led to touch their feet and pray for their walk. I kept praying that this be real to them and that they never let it go. Two of those gentlemen went inside and got baptized that evening.

I cannot explain how my heart starts beating rapidly and I feel overwhelmed when I let go and pray. Sometimes I feel like I am going to just drop to the ground. But that would be so bad if I spend my last breath while I am praying for someone else or while I am dancing for Him?

During the tithes and offerings portion a gentleman said, "Ladies, lift your purses in the air. Men, lift your wallets in the air." Honestly, the first thought was, "He's going to ask us to Dig Deeper for the offering money." However, to my surprise he said, "I am going to pray a blessing over your finances." So, I lifted my purse in the air, and as he was praying, I was saying, "ABBA, you have already blessed my finances and provided for me all my life. All I ask is for You to help me be wise with my finances and be a good steward!"

The following Monday I went to work, and while I was working, I kept feeling overwhelmed by His Love. I stopped what I was doing, and I posted a message on Facebook about how awesome God is and that every time we appreciate HIS blessings and give Him thanks, He blesses us more.

I left work a little early as I had to make two stops to drop off collected donations for the holidays. When I got back in my car, I saw an email from my lawyer's office. The email said that the Chapter 13 plan would soon be final and approved. However, the fee agreed upon would be $250 less a month!

Yes, out of my entire debt -1/3 of the debt was wiped away! I was amazed that, once again, the Lord had given me a huge blessing. I sat there and cried. I immediately had to call and tell Marilyn and a couple other people this story! You see, the more we share testimonies and praise Him for the works He has done the more, He will consider doing for us.

The following day as I was walking Precious, I was thinking about this blessing and I realized this fact: God did not wipe away my debt. He knew that I wanted to do right and pay off my debt, because His Word says we should not have outstanding debt. He wiped away 1/3 for the amount I owed. That added up to the two lawyer fees and the accrued interest of the debt, leaving me to pay my original debt.

See God is so intricate with everything He does. Everything is tightly intertwined and precise. He could have wiped away the whole debt. He could have made me pay the whole debt. But He allowed me to have a break on the added fees while I continued to pay the debt I created. I trusted Him completely and I see His Hand in all my blessings.

As I finish up this chapter the word that just came in to my mind is "Tithe." Do you tithe? In the past several years, since I began tithing correctly and cheerfully, I have seen blessing after blessing. I know He is always taking care of me and I never want for anything.

Bring the whole tithe into the storehouse, that there may be food in my house. Test me in this," says the LORD Almighty, "and see if I will not throw open the floodgates of heaven and pour out so much blessing that there will not be room enough to store it. **Malachi 10**

The LORD will open the heavens, the storehouse of his bounty, to send rain on your land in season and to bless all the work of your hands. You will lend to many nations but will borrow from none. **Deuteronomy 28:12**

I urge you to give it a try. You may say, "I have bills, I cannot afford to tithe 10%." I say, "You can't afford NOT to tithe.".

Everything we have is from God. You can tell me that you worked very hard to earn that income. But I say, "Who woke you every day and gave you strength to go to work? Who provided you with the job opportunities? Who protected you while you were working?"

I gave it a try myself several years ago, thinking I would not be able to do it faithfully. However, I surprised myself. And I can honestly say that He provides for all my needs. When I think I cannot pay a bill, I will inexpertly receive money from another source without even asking for it.

It is not only a command to tithe, it is an honor to do so. Give it a try.

You see, not only I, but many people have been saying what God has been communicating to them. He really is gathering His people.

In the beginning of March, just before this COVID19 hit, I was in church at PenTab. They were having praise and worship. My mind came to my son, James, who is about to be released from prison again. He is 36 and has spent his life in and out of the system. All of a sudden, I went into a full-blown spiritual warfare session while standing there. I had no clue what they were singing anymore. This went on for a few minutes, and when I opened my eyes, the screens had a picture of a man standing with his arms wide open for the Lord and the congregation was singing, "Don't know how You did it, but You made a way." I was blown away by this interaction and communication. God just has a way of letting us know He is here and HE is listening.

A week later I had a dream two nights in a row about my Grandma-Phine (Dad's mom). And then I had a dream about my Dad. The next day at temple, as I was praying and the dreams came to mind. I said, "OK, Lord, who am I supposed to pray for? Joanne, Her children? Beverly's children?" And in my mind, I heard LOUD and clear, "NO, James, concentrate on James." As tears rolled down my face, I started praying again for my son.

I have no idea what God has planned for this 37-year-old man, who spent his life since age 12 in and out of programs and prison. But I continue to pray that James will turn his life to God and that God will turn his life around and bless him with peace, a job, and stability. I pray for James' heart and for peace of mind. And I pray for the safety of all those he comes in contact with, because I have heard some of the things he has done out on that street. So as a mother and a strong, serious child of the Most-High GOD -I put my son and all that accompanies him in the Palms of God's Mighty Hands. And I rest in Him.

April 11, 2020: Four weeks in to this COVID-19 crisis. We are in isolation – being quarantined to our homes except for work or getting essentials. We must wear masks wherever we go. Some people have children or family in their homes. Others have no one. Because G works from 6 am and comes home well after 7 pm, I am alone most of the day. I do thank God I have my little Precious to occupy my day, and it gives me the push I need to walk several times a day.

I could have, and should have, taken the time to write this book and possibly complete it by now. However, words are not coming, and I seem to avoid the computer. I know it is the enemy, and I am certain my God is stronger and will definitely give me the words to finish this book. I don't want it to be just any book. I want it to be a book that people will love to read. I don't want them to see me, Lisa B., in this book. I want to glorify God and show how powerful and committed our God is.

You see, in 2012, I stopped going to temple for more than two years. I started hanging out at the club with my husband. Drinking, enjoying the music and looking forward for the next Friday night to go out again became my habit. Hubby did not pay a lot of attention to me or take me anywhere. He would always be gone for hours at a time leaving me home. So, when he started taking me to the club on Friday nights, I was thrilled.

I loved the music and dressing up all pretty. Hubby still was very standoffish with me while we were together. While other couples held each other and danced, he stood either in front of me or behind me while listening to the music and looking around. I always felt like he was looking at other girls and thinking of them. I felt like he was not interested in me at all. I knew he loved me, but due to his pride, he could not bring himself to hold me or show affection. However, I made myself accept the circumstances and be satisfied that at least chose to bring me. I continued to go every weekend, and I enjoyed getting dressed up and listening to the music.

Shortly after my 50th birthday, someone that should have been his past, came into our life, and cut right into the middle of our marriage, and he let it happen. If he were stronger, he could have set the whole thing straight, and we would all be happy and friendly today. But no, he left me alone many times to go spend time with his family at her home.

In fact, in 2015, when we were about to get divorced, we were discussing the issues and in the midst of talking things out he said, "I never cheated on you." and I said, "Yes, you did, every time you left me alone on a holiday or an evening to go hang out over there you cheated on me. Cheating does not mean just having sex with someone else."

So, after ten months of this behavior from him, he was still taking me to the club every Friday and guess what? I let my guard down. I started liking the attention I was getting from another man. I do not need to write a whole book about it, but you know where the story goes from there.

So needless to say, temple took a back burner to my new club life. I felt like a hypocrite, so instead of turning back to God, I turned in my dance garments and stopped the altar prayer ministry. Shortly after I just stopped going to temple. It was easier that way than to answer questions when people would come up and ask, "How you doing Lisa? Why aren't you dancing?"

I missed temple during that time, and I never forgot about God. God sure did not give up on me. I prayed regularly and begged forgiveness often and even heard when HE was giving me messages. My God held me so tight that I did not get far. I went a little too far -but He was right there pulling me out of the drowning waters.

In 2015, I started going back to temple after being drawn back by watching a video on Facebook about the Passover Seder and seeing posts from my TAK friends. I had stopped going to the club and stopped the other behavior before returning. When I started going back to temple, I took my time, not rushing to be a part of any ministry. I took time to speak with God and hear from Him and give it all to Him. Slowly I started getting involved in Sisterhood, then the dance ministry and then back on the Altar Prayer ministry. Slowly, I reconnected with my TAK friends and got many more over the past few years.

Be Still and Know that I am God; I will be exalted among the nations; I will be exalted in the earth!

Psalm 46:10

I am going somewhere with this, so bear with me! My neighbor Winsome invited me to a tea party at her church.

that the most important thing to do will be to fall on our knees and seek His Face.

If I had not gone back to temple and started going to PenTab last year, I would not be this strong in my faith. I am so thankful to our ABBA that He has kept me on a tight leash and has equipped me for a time such as this. While we are locked in our houses, we are making the most of the situation. I reach out daily via phone, Facebook, text and all that I can to give encouraging scriptures to anyone who will listen.

May 28, 2020: Wow. Where did the time go? The Lord put this book in my heart to write, He equipped me and I was doing so well. Then I had surgery and took 8 weeks to heal. I thought I would write more during my time at home, but I did not feel well at all, so I took the time to recover on my recliner. I started back to work on February 28th and not even two weeks later the world was turned upside down with COVID-19!

In the blink of an eye the entire world has changed. Everything was locked down and we were at a standstill. No work, no church, no parks or beaches, no visiting family, no one allowed to go in to the hospital to visit anyone, doctors' offices closed, surgeries postponed, no touching, no hugging, and everyone must wear facemasks.

The world was put in a Time-Out!

Plenty of time on my hands, yet I could not bring myself to write another paragraph in this book. I know the enemy tried to stop what the Lord started. However, for me it was just a break and the words will come out.

The great benefit from this time out is that people are getting back to basics. Whether they keep the basics in the next phase is yet to be seen. However, I pray the basics stay in my heart. In fact, a couple of weeks ago I was driving to Publix grocery store and I saw that for some reason Old Time Pottery store had their doors open and I immediately thought, "Wow, Old Time Pottery is open, I should just go mosey around there for a little while to kill some time." Immediately I thought, "Lisa, are you crazy, did you not learn anything? You do not need anything in that store!" I think that was my first lesson in living my new life where just popping in to the stores to kill time is no longer a habit.

Most churches and temples have gone on LIVE feeds on YouTube and Facebook. So, people can watch the messages right from home. And though it is not the same as going in person and seeing the friendly faces you are always used to seeing, it is more personal because it is just you and The Lord, in your living room.

I made it a point for Saturday temple service and Sunday morning PenTab service to get dressed (not in finest Sunday best clothes, but at least out of my pajamas), to brush my hair and put on makeup.

The Word became my entire focus. I was watching Pentecostal International's Wednesday night Bible study and their Sunday morning service, along with watching temple's Friday and Saturday services. Then there were the groups that would gather together to encourage each other on group chats. I was blessed with our "Quaranteam" made up of the Sisterhood committee. We made a vow to meet at 9 pm every night on WhatsApp to study scripture. In the past two months we have bonded, shared, studied, laughed, and cried together and encouraged each other. We share encouraging texts, scriptures, and songs throughout the day.

July 29, 2020: COVID-19 is still rampant in our world. Who would have imagined living this life isolated and unable to hug our loved ones?

It is strange how easy it is to get distracted from the task at hand. GOD gave me the task write this book. I have prayed about it over and over. I have picked it up and written with the belief that someone will be put in my life to edit and assist me with coordinating it.

In June we were told we would be back to work full time. I scolded myself over and over for the time that I wasted. Even though I sat in my house day after day, I could not bring myself to concentrate nor could I find words to write. God had given me all the time in the world to write and the words would not come.

On July 22nd, a Wednesday morning, I was on my knees giving thanks, praying for my family and friends, and putting the day in His Hands. All of a sudden, I started talking to God about the book! I said, "God, I wasted all that time that You gave me to write. You put us in TIME out and I froze! Can You please help me be more disciplined, to spend my time wisely, and give me the words I need for task You have given me?"

I did not ask Him to create more time for me. I asked Him to let me use my time wisely. But guess what? That morning when I went to work, my boss said, "We are back in Phase 1, and we are going to have the 3-day work week again." My thoughts immediately went to the prayer on my knees that morning. I am vowing to spend my time wisely, to take the time to sit and be still with Him, to take time to talk with Him, to read His Word, to pray for the words and messages, and to take the time to put all of it down on paper for the world to see. Yes, I will share with all that we are to "Honor the Glory of His Love."

Can you believe that once again, He answered that prayer on the same day? It is so amazing when He turns around and answers your prayers right away! This book is important to Him. He has given me the task. He is giving me all the great testimonies and praise reports to write. So, His perfect Will be done that I get this message out.

What am I thankful for about this COVID-19 Pandemic?

I have learned that COVID-19 is a Season necessary for growth. My life has actually changed a lot since March. I am sure this is true for everyone. In the blink of an eye there was so much uncertainty thrown at us. However, through it all I continue to hang tight to the hem of His garment. I am spending so much more time with Him and for Him. Yes, I used to pray on my knees every morning. Yes, I danced and praised Him every week at temple. Yes, I talked to Him often. But did I sit still in His Presence often enough? Did I read and understand the Word as I should? In these areas I was seriously lacking. I love Him, trust Him, and reach out to Him often. But now, there is such a deeper intensity in my relationship with Him and with those around me!

Thursday Prayer and Fasting: Our Sheshtas decided that we needed to take this up a notch. We were going to dedicate Thursdays to fast and pray for many different topics. I honestly had never fasted before. I did not know if I could do it. In fact, the first Thursday I was in the hospital, so I did not fast, and the second Thursday I completely forgot about it. Therefore, I was determined on the third week to take the fasting on Thursdays serious, and make it an integral part of my week.

[14]Consecrate a fast, Call a sacred assembly; Gather the elders And all the inhabitants of the land Into the house of the LORD your God, And cry out to the LORD. [15]Alas for the day! For the day of the LORD is at hand; It shall come as destruction from the Almighty. **Joel 1:14-15**

I wake up in the morning and pray on my knees in my room. I walk Precious and talk to the Lord as we are walking. I have music playing quietly as I write in my book, I sing and pray while cleaning up the house. I make an appointed time to lift the names of each of the children on our list. I listen to The Blessing Song and dance in my house. I also, do not touch food or turn on the television until after 2:30 pm.

20 So Jesus said to them, "Because of your unbelief; for assuredly, I say to you, if you have faith as a mustard seed, you will say to this mountain, 'Move from here to there,' and it will move; and nothing will be impossible for you.   21 However, this kind does not go out except by prayer and fasting." Matthew 17:20-21

116

I started back to work full time on October 5th. The week was so hectic with everyone trying to be back in the 5-day work week mode. In fact, that Friday morning I realized I completely missed the Thursday fast. I did not feel convicted like I had committed a sin or did something horrible. In fact, I just missed my time alone with the Lord. So, I vowed that I would seek ways to adjust my Thursdays to have more time for Him in the midst of a busy schedule.

The following Thursday I arrived to work early, since I was still driving a friend to and from work every day. I took my phone and my prayer list out in to the back yard behind my office and spent 45 minutes with music praying and talking with Him. I was actually dancing and bowing down while I was praying. It was just me and my ABBA!

As I was singing and looking up at all the windows and praying for all of our 300 residents, I thought if anyone sees me down here, they will think I've lost my mind. They will ask my boss, "What is Lisa doing out in the back yard?" Later that morning a resident was walking by and said hello to me. "Was that you out in the back yard this morning?" He asked. "Yes," I replied, "Don't think I've lost it, I was just listening to worship music and praying for you and all the other residents." That got a smile out of him.

I also dedicated the lunch time to my Thursday schedule. No television, The Staff usually gathers in the TV room with our lunches and watch the Young and the Restless. I went outside, parked my truck in the shade and sat on the back of my truck for the hour.

I learned that fasting was not just to give up food. While that takes a lot of discipline to give up food, that is not the purpose of fasting. You need to spend the quality time alone with the Lord to seek His Presence, seek His guidance, read His Word, to be still with Him, to pray for all your petitions, and give thanks to Him. You won't feel His Presence or hear His Words if you have the day-to-day noise in your ears. So, turn on the music and worship and dance in your house with Him! Sit outside in the fresh air if possible. Be still with Him.

One evening during our Sheshtas group study, Rebbitzen chose the song "Reside" from Sue Samuels for our evening song. As I listened to the song my mind ran to my fasting time and I realized this was my fast. My fast is "More than a Visitation it is a Sweet Inhabitation." That is what the Lord wants from us - Sweet Inhabitation.

Oh, how I thank Him for this experience and time for me to grow with Him and with my sisters. Remember, I said in a previous chapter that for most of my life I did not like to be alone at all. I truly enjoy my alone time now, because I know I am NEVER EVER alone. He is with me, and He will never leave me nor forsake me. So, I bask in His Presence as often as I can.

The *Lord* is near to *All* who call on *Him.*

Psalm 145:18

Chapter 13

Abuse is Not Ok! You Are Special to GOD

I was not going to go here. However, it weighed heavily on my mind the other day so I decided that I should include this subject, because someone just may need to hear it.

Abuse is NOT OK! Physical, mental, or verbal. People that use these tactics have such low self-esteem that they throw their frustrations out on those closest to them. No one has the right to touch you, hurt you, talk down to you, or make you feel worthless. God created you with a purpose and you are very special to Him.

> **⁶ Do you not know that you are the temple of God and *that* the Spirit of God dwells in you? If anyone defiles the temple of God, God will destroy Him. For the temple of God is holy, which *temple* you are. *1 Corinthians 3:16-17***

My first marriage was full of abuse. I will not bore you with elaborate stories of my painful first marriage. However, I was verbally, mentally, and physically abused from the age of fifteen right through the entire marriage. When he spoke to me with those vulgar words it would always make me cringe. I was always embarrassed wherever we went, because he was very loud and would argue over everything without respect for me or for those around us.

Verbal and Mental: He was constantly calling me names and yelling at me every day for no real reasons. He would tell me I was so fat no one would want me if I left him. In one breath

When my children were a little older, I enrolled at ATI Career Training Institute where I received a certificate in Business Administration. I worked at ATI as a receptionist part time while I was attending, and after graduation they hired full time. From there I was blessed to get a job at an HUD subsidized elderly housing community. It was a clerical position for the first two years, and then I was promoted to Assistant Manager with many responsibilities. I have been working there for the past twenty-seven years.

I remember one time when I just started the classes for the city program, I was in a doctor's office waiting for an appointment. I was watching the receptionist scrambling around performing all her responsibilities with ease and self-assurance. I thought, "Wow, I wish I could be that efficient." Then one day, many years later, I was busy running the copier with the 300 copies of the monthly newsletter, which I create from front to back, and I was doing something else while the copier was running, when my thoughts brought me back to that insecure Lisa in the doctor's office wishing she had skills and self-assurance.

I brought this baggage of low self-esteem right with me well into my second marriage. I cannot even tell you when the insecurities disappeared completely. I am proud to say they are gone and I know I am loved. I guess once I started trusting that the Lord brought me here for a purpose and that He loves me just as He loves anyone else, the insecurities faded way without me even realizing.

Now I know: JESUS LOVES ME THIS I KNOW FOR THE BIBLE TELLS ME SO!

My message in this is that you are loved! You deserve to live a life free from abuse. If you have to move out of your luxury house and live with your three children in an efficiency to escape abuse, then I recommend you do so. I lived with my three children in an efficiency while I went to school full time and worked full time. If I can do it then I know you can do it.

The LORD has appeared of old to me, saying, Yes, I have loved you with an everlasting love: therefore, with loving kindness have I drawn you. Jeremiah 31:3

"He will wipe away every tear from their eyes, and death shall be no more, neither shall there be mourning, nor crying, nor pain anymore, for the former things have passed away." Revelation 21:4

My children's father and I still talk to this day. People always say, "You still talk to him? I would hate him." I know God blessed me since before I can remember with a forgiving heart. I never hated anyone in my lifetime. I may never forget that I was hurt, and I will definitely be alert to keep myself from getting hurt by that person again. However, I am quick to forgive. I will always love and pray for my first love, who is the father of my children. I don't wish him unhappiness.

I did not want to write about my first marriage in this book and believe me when I say that I have been very sparing with the stories. However, I kept thinking that it needed to be addressed to help others.

So, to that woman or man out living in this situation right now I say to you:

- Abuse is Not Ok – The first black eye is one too many
- Your body is the temple of the Most High God -don't let anyone abuse it.
- Take charge of your destiny
- You alone can take steps to a positive future
- Know that You ARE LOVED! ***Yes, I have loved you with an everlasting love; Jeremiah 31:3***
- Your Sar Shalom -Prince of Peace is with you. Get on your knees and talk with Him and ask Him to surround you with His Perfect Peace.

Praying as I close this chapter that The Lord will touch hearts and lead them to a peaceful prosperous life filled with His joy.

Chapter 14

Friends Along the Way

Muchi - June 17, 2020: For quite a while I had been having symptoms of a racing heart. I went to the heart doctor in January for a check-up. Two years before this, I had gone to the doctor's office, because I was drooling a little and feeling like something wasn't quite right. They did an EKG and then called the ambulance to rush me to the hospital. The hospital kept me for two days and they believed it was a small TIA. I never really followed through with this. I took the medicine they gave me for about a year and stopped on my own.

Recently, I started having episodes where my heart was racing or I would drool a little. I decided not to go to the doctor, because I could not afford another ambulance bill if they decided I needed to go to the hospital. Instead, I drove to the emergency room to be checked out. They kept me overnight for observation.

When they brought me up to my room the curtain was closed, but I could hear my roommate talking to her visitor. She was talking loudly, so I could hear her entire conversation. She was going through situations with family, and she longed to separate herself from any dramas. The things she was telling her visitor were exactly the same things our Sheshtas group was discussing on our Tuesday night zoom the previous day! I did not want to tell her that I heard her entire conversation, but oh, how I wanted to tell her this was the same thing we were discussing.

1Therefore if you have any encouragement from being united with Christ, if any comfort from his love, if any common sharing in the Spirit, if any tenderness and compassion, 2then make my joy complete by being like-minded, having the same love, being one in spirit and of one mind. 3Do nothing out of selfish ambition or vain conceit. Rather, in humility value others above yourselves, 4not looking to your own interests but each of you to the interests of the others. 5In your relationships with one another, have the same mindset as Christ Jesus: Philippians 2:1-5

Friends
make the
world
beautiful.

<u>RIP My friend Casey- August 2020</u>: I just heard the news that my good friend Casey passed away this morning. As the tears flood from my eyes, I realize that I need to share the story of my friendship with Casey.

I started working at B'nai B'rith Apartments in 1994. I was a 33-year-old single mother driving 40 minutes to work daily. Life was not really easy and was still very much full of drama.

Casey was an elderly resident there. She was actually one of the first residents to move in to the building in 1987. Casey's life was not peaceful due to spousal circumstances that I won't get in to. However, you would never know this, because Casey always greeted people with the most beautiful smile and shiny eyes full of love. She had this peaceful glow with her all the time. Every time I was near Casey, I would be filled with this peaceful spirit.

I had not attended church regularly for many years, and like many, I did not want to hear people telling me to go to church or to repent. I believed in God, I prayed to God daily, and I did not need church. Casey never told me the things I did not want to hear. Casey always said, "God Loves you, Lisa, I am praying for you, and your family, Lisa." And I would always smile and say, "Thank you, I love God too, and I thank you for the prayers."

Casey kept my family and I in her daily prayers. I knew when she would say that she was praying that she was telling the truth. These were not just words from someone promising to pray and then forgetting. She actually thought of me all the time and prayed for me. I would give God thanks for her often.

129

As I started going to temple and getting stronger in my relationship with God, Casey saw the difference though I never mentioned my changes to her. We would always stop in the hallway and talk about Him and share some awesome recent testimony. When we got together you could feel HIS Presence so thick around us. It was a beautiful bond that only GOD could give us.

One morning I was sitting at my desk and Casey popped in my mind. I called her and asked how she was doing. It crossed my mind and I said, "Do you mind if I come up for a few minutes?" Mind you, I never do that with any residents. It just came out of my mouth! Casey said, "Sure, Ralph is not home, come on up." As I was walking away from my desk, my eyes fell on the bottle of anointing oil that was given to me as a gift months before. I grabbed the oil and put it in my pocket. Once in the apartment we were chatting for a short while and we decided to pray. I asked if I could use the oil. While we were praying and anointing that apartment, we could feel the Presence of the Holy Spirit so strong. We were hugging and laughing at the amazing gift of His Presence. The peace that followed was so beautiful.

Whenever we saw each other in the hallway we would have a praise report to tell each other. I cannot explain this relationship better than to say that GOD was the entire beginning, circle, and center of this friendship. We were always feeling when the other was in need of prayer without even asking.

After her husband passed away Casey began to get ill. Cancer and lung problems took its toll on her for many years. Breathing was difficult to say the least. However, she just kept on going like a champ, praising His Name all the years of her life.

I was home one Saturday morning, and I was sitting downstairs watching television. For some reason I walked up to my room, pulled an older Bible off my shelf, and sat on my bed. I had never done anything like that before. So, I opened up the Bible, shifted through pages and I said, "God, what do you have for me?" All of a sudden, Casey popped in my mind. I started praying some very serious warfare prayers for Casey though I had no idea what was going on. I said, "God, You know what Casey needs and what is going on, I am trusting You alone with my friend that You have her right NOW in the palms of Your Mighty Hands." I don't know what else I prayed but it was all for Casey.

I was shaking from the overwhelming experience, and I thought to myself, "Wow, that was so strange, I am going to have to call Casey Monday to tell her and see what she is going through." But then again, I am very impatient and could not wait until Monday, so I looked her number up. I called and said, "Casey, this is Lisa, I am just calling to see how you are. Casey replied, "I am ok now, but ten minutes ago I thought I was dying!" Seems her heart was racing, and she could not breathe. She was having some sort of episode and she started to pray -then God put her Prayer Warriors to work I guess, and I am so proud to have been called to task. It was such an amazing experience from the Lord.

I would always pray with Casey out loud and say, "ABBA, please hold my friend tight and don't let her feel pain. ABBA, please let Casey always have breath to sing to You, pray to You, and share the Good News until the day You decide to call her home. Let her praise You as long as she has breath,

The funeral was scheduled for the following Saturday morning via the internet due to COVID-19. I did not plan on watching as I had my duties on the Dance Ministry and also it was my week to assist the altar Prayer Ministry. I decided that I had already said my goodbyes.

The Friday before I had spent most the day working on this book. I saved it and sent what I believed was the saved file to my email so I could work on it at home over the weekend. When I pulled the file up on Saturday morning there was an old file attached to the email. It was a file without all the changes from the previous day. I prayed that I did not lose all my work, and I decided I would take a ride up to my workplace in Deerfield after temple services to check my computer for the newest version.

I went to temple and told all who would listen about Casey's last night. After service I was in the Altar Prayer closet waiting for people to come in for prayer. Not one person came to us for prayer. Absolutely no one came! That has never happened to me. We are usually there for quite a while praying after a service and no one came. This is where the story of timing comes in.

I left temple and drove straight to Deerfield. I went in my office and to my grateful surprise, the file on the computer was the newest version with all my hard work saved on it. I was thrilled. I sent that version to my email, which oddly enough was the only version in my document file, and I headed home to get some writing done.

As I left the office, I decided I would go down Dixie Highway to make a stop on the way home. To get to Dixie Highway, I turned down the cemetery street which is right near the building. When I turned down the street, I saw a freshly dug hole and men sitting at a table and cars lining up. Traffic was slow, so I slowly made my way past them. The moment I saw this I realized this was Casey's funeral procession.

I pulled over a couple of houses past the cemetery with tears just talking to God. I wondered if I should go around and try to join the line but decided against getting in the crowd. I sat there saying thank You to God for Casey in my life when all of a sudden, her hearse pulled slowly around the corner and made its final stop! God allowed me to witness Casey's final ride whether I chose to or not!

His Hands entirely! The wrong file sent home and no one in line for prayer making the timing of this all possible. He made sure I got to witness Casey's hearse pulling up to her final resting place. Even now, though the tears flow from my eyes, there is joy in my heart. I give thanks to the most Awesome God who gave me the most beautiful friend that anyone could ever ask for. We were more like "God Friends" than just good friends.

How do you thank Him for such a beautiful gift? You write about the testimony in your book for the world to see His Goodness!

Chapter 15

Short Stories with Great Meaning

His Light Shines In Us:

My sister-in-law, Brunilda (from my first marriage) and I were out running errands one day. Her husband had passed away, so I was going over every weekend to help her with her books and making sure everything was copacetic with her finances as he always paid the bills, and she was at a loss.

This particular day we were on our way to the store. There was a woman selling watermelons on the side of the road. I pulled over to the side to buy a watermelon.

When I reached to hand this woman the money, there was this powerful flow of energy that went right through both of us. We looked at each other amazed and then started talking to each other about the goodness of God. We hugged and said good bye when I left.

When I got back in my truck, I did not know what to say to Bruni, so I said, "Wow, that was strange!" Bruni was very emotional and she said to me, "No, it wasn't and I want what you have!"

She and I talked a lot about where I go to worship and how my life had changed since I started walking with the Lord. She even went to temple with me twice and loved it. However, then she got complications with her back and had to have another procedure, so she could not sit through a service.

After that procedure her life was different. She got dependent on pain killers and was always depressed. I did not see her often during that time, because she did not want visitors and was content to be locked up in her dark room with pain meds. Those pain meds have taken away so many of my family members through both death and drama.

Bruni was hit by a car a couple of years after this incident. She was in a coma and never woke up. When she was in the hospital, we were at her side praying and singing softly and her heart rate would go up. The nurses told us we had to sit quiet and not sing or talk because every time we were singing or praying, we were agitating her. I know she was touched by His Presence and was excited as she had tears in her eyes. So, I softly prayed and sang whenever the nurses were not in the room.

I witnessed her final moments with Jesus' holding her and saw when she let go with a relief on her face. However, the family kept her on the machine for a few more days so she could die on her birthday. This was not my call to make. I am just blessed that I witnessed her tears when we were praying and the look of relief when He wrapped His arms around her and called her home.

This is the message we have heard from Him and declare to you: God is light; in Him there is no darkness at all. 6 If we claim to have fellowship with Him and yet walk in the darkness, we lie and do not live out the truth. 7 But if we walk in the light, as he is in the light, we have fellowship with one another, and the blood of Jesus, his Son, purifies us from all sin <u>1 John 1:5-7</u>

Then Moses said to the LORD, "Please, Lord, I have never been eloquent, neither recently nor in time past, nor since You have spoken to Your servant; for I am slow of speech and slow of tongue." The LORD said to Him, "Who has made man's mouth? Or who makes Him mute or deaf, or seeing or blind? Is it not I, the LORD? "Now then go, and I, even I, will be with your mouth, and teach you what you are to say."

Exodus 4:10-12

For the next three nights I looked up ideas on what to speak about. Rabbi Joe had spoken of tithing the week before and explained to the members how important tithing was to keep the temple up and running. He asked the question: When someone is in the hospital or someone passed away, who is the first person we call to be there?

I had never given much thought to that. But yes, he was right, when Magic died, temple was there. In fact, Rabbi Joe was my first call. When Joey was in the hospital for a week in a coma, temple was there with prayers, food, and even assisted in fixing up my sisters' home, so he could go home to a clean and healthy environment. Whenever anyone in my family needed prayer, temple was there.

The message was so good that it stayed fresh in my mind and I included this message in my message. I spoke of the thorns on the ground when Adam and Eve ate from the fruit and how Jesus wore those thorns on His crown when He died for us. Not only did God use me, but He equipped me mightily first and then used me. He tested me, and for a brief moment, the enemy almost got me by throwing fear on my mind. But I was stronger in my love and faith for the Lord, and I feel pretty confident that I made Him proud.

140

Many of my family members came to support me. They do not realize that more importantly than them supporting me was the fact that they were in church getting fed!!

I am so grateful that I was strong enough to say yes when the enemy had that fear in my mind along with the "no" on the tip of my tongue. From that moment on, when I ask God to equip me and use me mightily, I expect that He will be calling on me to do something for Him right away. No longer will I say no because of fear.

The Mask

June 4, 2020, I was standing in line at Publix. There was a young lady in line 6 feet in front of me with her mask on taking the groceries out of her basket to place on the counter. I was taking notice of her mask and how nice it fit and how it coordinated with her shirt. Then I thought, "She has beautiful eyes, it's a shame to hide her pretty face behind a mask."

Then all of a sudden, I thought, "Hmmmm, did God give us these masks to hide our faces?" Think about it:

- Some people won't go out with someone unless they look good.
- Many women hide their faces behind a mask of makeup.
- People are putting tattoos and ear piercings all over their face and body.
- People spend a lot of money on face lifts and body work.
- People get bullied and mocked because of their looks.
- The tone our skin color hinders people in so many various ways.

- If someone has a scar it affects how people react to them.

The list goes on and on. Wow, ABBA, are You covering our faces for a reason other than to protect our health?

Charm is deceitful, and beauty is vain, but a woman who fears the Lord is to be praised. <u>**Proverbs 31:30**</u>

But the Lord said to Samuel, "Do not look on his appearance or on the height of his stature, because I have rejected Him. For the Lord sees not as man sees: man looks on the outward appearance, but the Lord looks on the heart." <u>**1 Samuel 16:7**</u>

<u>In His Hands</u>:

In September of 1999, I was in my bedroom one morning ironing and getting ready for work. I was barely listening to the television. Suddenly Benny Hinn said, "I am going to pray for all you mothers out there that have been praying for your children for years and you are tired and waiting for your prayers to be answered."

Now this would be me, as I was at a loss when it came to my two sons. Our lives were full of drama since 1994, when they became in involved with gang related activities. They were continually in and out of both programs and prison, for stealing cars, committing burglaries, and drug possession. I expected bad news daily. In fact, Jamie was in jail at the time and Magic was still out on the streets hanging out, getting high, and stealing.

Benny Hinn said, "Parents lift your hands and pray with me," and I did just that. He prayed and my hands lifted in the air as I repeated his words. *"Father, I am tired. I have been praying for my sons for so long. This battle is your battle, Lord, not mine! Please, Lord, have your way with them. Do not let them wander the streets lost, confused, doing drugs, and stealing with the gang, Lord. I have been praying for years and years, Lord. I place them In Your Hands right now! In the name of Jesus, I pray."*

It was less than a week later that God called my son Magic home where he could find eternal peace. This is not the outcome I was praying for. But God heard my prayers. and I am sure God knows best.

> **Cast all your anxiety on Him because he cares for you.**
> **1 Peter 5:7**

Don't Ignore The Nagging Thoughts:

In 1990, my sister Beverly and her husband, Jose, were taking a trip. I had their daughter, Elizabeth, and son, Joey, staying with me during their time away. One night, I specifically remember the clock showed 11:30 pm, when I was getting ready to go to sleep. Those days when I went to sleep, I always prayed the simple, "Now I lay me down to sleep" prayer and then I would name all the names in my family before I finally said, "In the name of the Father, the Son, and The Holy Spirit, AMEN." That was my typical every night prayer since I was a child.

I finished my prayers and was just getting ready to drop to sleep. My mind went on Beverly and Jose and I thought, "Oh

I had a friend named Carole. She worked at the front desk and I was very close with her. I always called her mom. She was a Jewish lady. When she was in the hospital during her final days, I went to visit her with Marilyn. Marilyn was talking to her about Jesus and Carole looked at her and said, "I believe He is real." And Marilyn asked her what would make her believe that. Carole told us that a priest would visit her roommate and when he was praying, she could feel His Presence. So, we prayed with Carole to accept Yeshua into her heart.

A couple of nights later Rabbi Joe and I visited Carole. We sat with her, talked with her, prayed with her, and sang for her. She had this peaceful look all night long. I promised her I would spend the next day with her as I took a vacation day with the purpose of spending it visiting her.

The next morning, I was driving to the rehab and I somehow had a gut feeling that that I was too late and that she had passed away. So, the entire drive I prayed, "Dear God, please don't let that bed be empty, let Carole be there, don't let that bed be empty." Imagine my relief when I saw her feet on the bed when I turned the corner.

There was a staff member sitting in in a chair in the corner reading a book. I said hello to her and walked right up to Carole's bed. I looked down at her peaceful face and turned to the woman and said, "Wow, she looks so peaceful." The woman said, "She's gone dear."

The woman must have thought I lost my mind because I burst into laughter. I turned to the woman and told her, "God really does have a sense of humor! I did not ask Him to let her be alive. I begged for Him not to let the bed be empty."

I truly believe He uses humor and the premonitions to soften the blows when they come my way. So, remember, be very careful whenever you word your prayers. He is very literal and precise! If you pray for someone who is sick, ask for healing. Don't ask Him to not let the bed be empty!

> *And whatever you ask in prayer, you will receive, if you have faith."* **Matthew 21:22**

Sweet Surprise:

One day I decided to take a walk on the beach before work. The weather was so cool, breezy, and beautiful. I was feeling great. I walked briskly up and down the beach singing and talking to Him for over an hour.   My hands were lifted up and I couldn't stop thanking Him. I was giving Him thanks for my day, thanks for my family, thanks for this and thanks for that. I was praying for everyone that came to mind.

Whenever I walk on the beach, I keep my eye open for a pretty shell to take home. It was near time to head back to my car, and I said to myself, "Oh, no pretty shells today?" All of a sudden, I looked up and said, "ABBA, I don't need a shell. There is no shell that can compare to Your love for me!" As soon as I the words came out of my mouth, I looked down and saw the prettiest purple and white shell with another little white shell attached, and it just looked like God holding me!

He is right on time! With Sweet Surprises –Right on time!

Every good and perfect gift is from above, coming down from the Father of the heavenly lights, who does not change like shifting shadows. <u>**James 1:17**</u>

Chapter 16

HE Talks To Me

Below you will find a few more stories about some of the many times in my life that I know GOD spoke directly to me. He is definitely talking to us and we need to be open to hear from Him. I pray that through my stories you will see that with God nothing is too small for Him. He speaks to us in many ways. He may speak boldly into your thoughts. He may touch you with a message spoken at service that you know is just for you. Someone may call you out of the blue with a message that will blow you away with the timing of your circumstance.

You must truly believe in Him and keep your heart and your ears open to Him. Then, and only then, will you definitely hear from Him.

The Lord Wants You To Have Joy:

In 1994, I was attending ATI Career Training center. I had a teacher named Jon who invited me to go to his church, "The 4th Avenue Church of God." I visited the church on several occasions before I found my home at Temple Aron Hakodesh.

Once several years later Jon invited me to the church as they were having a guest pastor. During the service the pastor, who was standing in front speaking, started walking up and down to different areas of the church. He was walking straight up to random people and he was touching the people while praying in tongues and they were falling to the ground.

I, the control freak that I am, did not want to fall down. Taking my mind from that fact I started focusing on praying for others. I began praying for the person in front of me who appeared to be homeless. I had my hands up and was saying to the Lord, "Lord, bless this man and meet his needs. Suddenly I was saying, "Lord don't let the pastor come here, please don't let the pastor come here." Just as those prayers went up to the Lord, the pastor, who was walking around the room to everyone else, went up to the altar, pointed to me and shouted, "YOU IN THE PRINT DRESS COME UP HERE NOW." I walked up to him, he put his hand to my forehead and said, "NO WORDS NECESSARY," and I fell to the floor filled with the Holy Spirit.

I lay there in His Presence and couldn't stop laughing with tears pouring down my face. When I got up, I told the pastor that I told the Lord not to let Him call on me. The pastor said, "The Lord wants your heart to be full of Joy and Laughter."

May the God of hope fill you with all joy and peace as you trust in Him, so that you may overflow with hope by the power of the Holy Spirit. Romans 15:13

Modesty:

In 2004, I had the gastric bypass operation to lose weight. Even as I went through the procedure, I never imagined that I would really lose a lot of weight. I was so excited at the results and happily went shopping for a new wardrobe. I had quite a nice wardrobe. I had clothes to wear to temple on Saturdays, clothes to wear to work, and play clothes. Unfortunately, I was in my mid 40s and most of the work and play clothes that I bought were catered more to younger ladies.

One weekend I was walking through a Publix grocery store, and a couple that I knew from temple came up to me and said hello. Quick thinking, I nonchalantly held my shirt closed, had a brief conversation with them, and went on my merry way. All of a sudden, the thought rang loudly in my head, "If you had to hold your shirt closed to say hello to them then you have no business wearing it!"

Likewise, also that women should adorn themselves in respectable apparel, with modesty and self-control, not with braided hair and gold or pearls or costly attire,

1 Timothy 2:9

The Message of Our Father's Love:

It was 2010. At that time, I was in "walking mode." I walked every day, rain or shine for an hour. I walked around the block, at a park, at the beach, wherever my mind told me to walk that day. One day I decided the beach was a perfect spot for my walk. While walking my mind went to my circumstances. I was getting so tired of always feeling lonely. Yes, I was married to a good man. However, he was a hard worker who was out at 6 am and back home at 11 pm, even on the weekends. So, life at home was very lonely.

I walked fast and talked to God as always. I never usually went in the water when I walked, but the water looked so inviting that I decided to go for a swim. I was enjoying my time in the warm calm water. I looked around and saw all the other people in the water splashing, playing around, and laughing together. All of a sudden, I started crying desperately. I said, "GOD, I AM SOOOOO LONELY! I know I have family and friends, but I feel so alone!"

I got out of the water with tears in my eyes and walked to my towel. I looked down at my phone and I saw that I had a missed call from a lady I knew from temple. I wondered why she was calling me. I hit call back button to see if she needed something.

She said, "Hello, Lisa. Don't think I am crazy, but God placed it in my heart to call you and to tell you that you are never alone, that He loves you, and He will never leave you!" WOW, WOW, WOW! Talk about being blown away! There is No coincidence to the timing of that phone call.

> *The LORD Himself goes before you and will be with you; he will never leave you nor forsake you. Do not be afraid; do not be discouraged.'* **Deuteronomy 31:8**

God loves us. He is right here holding each and every one of us in the palms of His Mighty Hands. We just need to believe. If we call on Him and be very still, we will feel His Presence.

Healing in Kneeling:

On Christmas Eve I left my house at 6:30 am, in a rush to get to Walmart before the crowds. I just had to buy two more gifts to complete my list. I was driving down Oakland Park Boulevard listening to Pastor Trevor Wallace on the radio, when I realized I forgot to get on my knees and pray before I left my house.

I spoke out loud to the LORD. "Lord, oh my, I was in such a hurry to get out the door that I didn't get on my knees in the room this morning, but I do love You and appreciate You, Lord."

When all of a sudden, I heard Pastor Trevor on the radio saying, "It's one thing to pray when you're on your way, but there is healing in kneeling. When you are on your knees, you are surrounded by God's angels and you have favor with God."

For whom the LORD loves He chastens, And scourges every son whom He receives. <u>Hebrews 12:6</u>

Show Me:

Recently, I was in church. During the praise and worship, I had my arms up and I was saying over and over "Thank You, Jesus, thank You, I love YOU, I love YOU."

Suddenly, a Bold, Loud, and Clear thought came right at me, "SHOW ME! It is easy to say I love you. Show Me!"

God's Timely Word:

I was in the bathroom and I was talking to God. I talk a lot to Him in there! I was asking God to remove some people from my life all together, because it hurt to even think about how much they hurt me. I no longer wanted to know anything about them, to hear from them, or for them to even hear or talk about me. I asked Him to remove them from my life completely, so I wouldn't hear hurtful things all the time from the wicked hearts.

After my trip to the restroom, I was talking with my coworker about being frustrated and that I didn't want these people in my life at all at all. A few minutes later I checked my phone to see that my friend Muchi sent me this message right out of the blue:

The timely message read: *"When you decide to walk on the water, you have to drown out the noise of those still sitting in the boat. Own your life. Take it back from the hands of the enemy and put it the Hands of God. Stop worrying over what people will think and follow what God has put in your heart. Don't let the world steal your confidence. Remember that you have been created on purpose by the Hand of God. He has a special, unique, wonderful plan for you. Go for it. Don't shrink back, conform, or live in fear."*

He's Preparing Us:

At temple, Priscila was dancing. I was standing there at my seat worshipping and the mask was making it difficult to breathe, and I was so hot. I lifted my hands, and crying out said, "Lord, please let us worship- let us take these masks off soon to worship without this mask." All of a sudden these words came boldly to my mind: "NO, MY DEAR, I CANNOT TAKE IT AWAY FROM YOU. I AM PREPARING YOU FOR SOMETHING ELSE. SOMETHING GREATER."

Stepping Out of My Comfort Zone:

I had it in my heart to lead the worship at our TAK Women Worship and the Word Sunday meeting. So, I crept out my comfort zone and volunteered. I had not sang being accompanied by a piano since I was a teenager in chorus. Linda, who was accompanying me on the keyboard, met with me several times to practice the songs.

The day before our event, I was practicing a song that I had not practiced before. I had to sing a portion of it in key higher than am used to singing. That entire day I practiced the song while doing my chores and every time I walked my Yorkie, Precious. I practiced it over and over again. I wanted it to be perfect and give my all to glorify Him.

I did not sleep much that night. I awoke at 4 am with the song, "Our God is an Awesome God" playing inside my head. I decided that I would sing that song at the close of the message along with the other three that I had chosen to open with.

I could not go back to sleep, so I went downstairs, sat on my chaise, and turned on the TV. The movie, "The Birds" by Alfred Hitchcock was on. I watched it for about 10 minutes and then I said to myself out loud, "Why are you watching this?" and I switched the channel.

I do not know what channel it was, and I did not recognize the gentleman on the screen. However, the minute it went to that channel the gentleman said, "Lift your hands and I am going to pray for you." So, I lifted my hands as he was praying, I was agreeing in prayer with him. When all of a sudden, I

The next day I was talking to G, who had already heard about the commotion. He said to me, "OH, my nose is itching, I am going to be in a fight!" I did not even remember saying that comment until he mentioned it. But I'll never forget that story. I am very careful not to repeat those folklores in jest.

The Knife:

One story I am not proud of, but I will tell it, so you can see the power of the tongue. When my husband and I were dating, we were going through a lot of difficulties. I did not know the Lord and did not seek Him for direction, so I always had drama and chaos.

One day I went early in the morning to the flea market with my sister-in-law. Along with my other purchases, I bought a kitchen knife. My sister-in-law asked me what I needed the knife for, and I jokingly said, "Oh, I guess I will just stab G." "That is not funny," she responded. "I'm JUST kidding!" I laughed.

Well, that very day G and I were in having some sort of disagreement and he came over to my house and we were arguing. He said something that tore my heart out and got in his truck. I was devastated and as I went to his window to say more, I looked over and saw a jack knife sitting in the console, I grabbed it and stabbed him in the arm. He got out of the truck and came in after me. I went in to my house and there on the counter was my new knife. I took that knife outside and slashed all four of his tires. He in-turn slashed all four of my tires. The following day my sister-in-law reminded me of the conversation we had.

You see, we must be very careful with our thoughts and our words. In fact, when I am on my knees in the morning, I try to remember to ask the Lord to let everything out of my mind and out of my mouth be pleasing to Him.

Set a guard over my mouth, LORD; keep watch over the door of my lips. <u>**Psalm 141:3**</u>

Chapter 18
Dreams and Visions

These pages are bits and pieces of dreams or visions I have had. They are in no particular order. I just feel they are important. One of the messages may be for you today. We should keep our eyes open wide, write down our dreams and pray about them.

I Will Honor the Glory of Your Love:

I dreamt there was a gathering of people worshipping and someone handed me paper and told me to write something on it. It seems we were creating a song. When I went to write the sentence, I had chosen for the song, I noticed the other lines were already filled with the sentences from other people.

Everyone had written the same thing. "I will honor the glory of Your love."

I woke up right after that with the words on my tongue and I spoke them out loud. I knew I needed to remember that sentence, so I picked up my phone and put it on the notepad so I would not forget.

That morning I was thinking about something that Claire and I were talking about the prior day. I had told her something that I saw, and she asked if I thought it was a vision of me thinking of the idea. I told her that I wasn't sure that it was something that I saw as they were practicing.

While I was eating breakfast, I decided I was going to talk to Claire about visions as I didn't think I had ever had a vision before. All of a sudden, I reached my hands up and said, "God, why have I never had visions? Give me visions if it be Your desire that I have them."

That day at work I was looking for something on my phone and I saw my notes about the dream in the middle of the night. I looked up verses for dreams and came up with Acts 2:17— Yes, HE does give me dreams. I have had several where I knew they were from Him. In fact, last week I sang a beautiful song in my dream, but when I woke up, I could not remember any of the words. That is why I wrote this note down with the one sentence from this last dream: "I will honor the glory of Your love."

(Glory= great beauty and splendor : magnificence)

For the next week after the two dreams, one of which I remembered and wrote on paper, I talked a lot with GOD. I asked Him, if it be His will, He would give me visions and let me be wise with the visions He gave me. That Tuesday night, I went to a TAK meeting called "A Night with the Ruach."

At the altar that night, I was just basking in His Presence, giving Him thanks, and trying to be quiet -listening to the music and trying very hard to quiet my mind. A beautiful lion came right up to my face (as if it were Precious or a kitty) and I could feel the fur in my face brushing my cheek. And I know He is right here protecting me: It was the most peaceful beautiful feeling that you could possibly imagine.

During the same evening Elder Francisco was speaking. When he quoted **Matthew 27:51** *"Then, behold, the veil of the temple was torn in two from top to bottom; and the earth quaked, and the rocks were split,"* my mind immediately came to the Pandemic and how people were frozen in panic for several days before they even started to get a grip. Then I thought of when there is a sudden storm or something is happening, our first instinct is to run to the window or turn on the television and stare in unbelief at the situation.

I realized at that moment that God wants us to always be ready! He wants our first instinct to be to <u>DROP</u> to our knees to seek His face and to seek His wisdom and guidance. Do this before we turn on the TV or run to look out the window.

This was an overwhelmingly powerful week full of experiences with His Presence.

<u>Going to See the King</u>:

I remember night several years ago, I woke up from this dream: I was in Jamaica. I was walking through the streets of Jamaica with hundreds of people, mostly children, walking with me. I was in front and we were singing over and over again, "Soon and very soon we are going to see the KING."

I woke up with an overwhelming feeling. I remember thinking, "Wow, that was a weird dream. A nice, but weird dream." When I went to dance practice, I told the Dance and Prayer ministry leader Arlene about the dream. She said, "Lisa, where is your husband from?" I said, "He's from Jamaica." She said, "Your husband is going to come to Salvation!"

Don't Look Away:

I was dreaming Jesus was walking down a winding road with a lot of people behind Him. There was a long haired scrubby looking guy who was mean and being a jerk. I said, "He is rotten." Then the guy touched Jesus and started walking behind Jesus with a whole new look. I said, "He is following Jesus; he isn't rotten anymore." Then I started moving a little slower and began looking at everything around me. When I turned back around, I couldn't see Jesus or the crowd as they had turned another way.

I was walking and running trying to catch up and find them. I was singing loudly, "Here I am Jesus, Your servant is following You, slow down Jesus, Your servant is following You." And then I saw Him. He slowed down and I got right up in front of the line. As we were walking, I told everyone "sing with me" and we were singing "Jesus Loves His Little Children."

The message I got from this dream was: The time is here and now. Don't get lost in the winding roads in life. Keep your eyes on Him. August 1, 2018

25Let your eyes look straight ahead; fix your gaze directly before you. 26 Give careful thought to the paths for your feet and be steadfast in all your ways. 27 Do not turn to the right or the left; keep your foot from evil. **Proverbs 4:25-27**

The Last Day:

On a Saturday morning I wrote, "Today I stand in overwhelming Awe. The songs and messages in temple seemed to go right along with my dream and message from last night. I realize that I really do not want to be in the position where I am scrambling around at the last minute to reach my family members."

The dream was about the final day running around trying to get family to pray and seek Him. I went to my daughter Alicia and said, "Please let's pray and ask Jesus into your heart," and she did. I was scrambling around to try and reach out to everyone in my family. People were all going about their business laughing and playing around like they had plenty of time. All of a sudden, a loud "HELLO" woke me up.

No one was in my room obviously, and my heart was racing. It was 2 am and I thought, "There is a message here, I have to write about this tomorrow." Then the nagging started: "NO, get up now, don't wait until tomorrow."

"No, go back to sleep silly, you can write it in the morning," I told myself. Finally, I heard, "GET UP NOW! Tomorrow might be too late!" So, I got up out of bed and went on the computer to post about the dream and asked in the post:

"Have you asked Jesus into your heart? Do you know He loves you no matter what you've done or where you are now? He is just waiting for you to ask Him and He has already forgiven. Even if you have asked Him into your heart, did you talk to Him today? He is reaching out to someone right now! Is it you? June 16, 2018

Evil Lurks Here:

For many years, I have had the practice to pray for the people who pop into my dreams. Whether it is a good dream or a bad dream, if I dream of someone whom I haven't seen or talked to, I feel God put them on my mind to take time to pray specifically for them.

One night recently I had a horrible dream. In the dream were my niece and nephews and the five daughters of two of my good friends (whom I call my nieces). In reality, this group of young adults are very close and have hung out together since they were young. If they are not busy working, you will find them all together at my sister-in-law's house.

The dream was so vivid. It is not like I had seen them recently. They just popped into my nightmare. It started out in a happy mellow mood and then it turned evil. My beautiful niece was smiling and laughing with me when all of a sudden, she pointed a gun at me. I pulled out a gun but did not want to hurt her. Then they all had guns and were looking for me. It seems that during the whole dream I was running, hiding, almost getting caught, and running again.

It was such a troubling dream, and I woke up with a dreadful feeling. While I know it was just a dream, I could not shake the feelings of dread for days. When I woke up, I prayed immediately for God to protect each of them and to let them know Him. Although they are always in my daily prayers, I feel God wanted me to pray for their lives to be free from the snares of the enemy.

The next Sunday while I was in church, a young lady got up to lead us all in the prayer requests when she burst out in prayer

Chapter 19

His Book- His Words -His Timing

At the beginning of this book, I shared how I walked up to the altar and placed this book in His Hands asking Him to equip me and to put people in my path to assist me with the production of this book. I had never written or published anything. Yet, I continued to write the book with faith and decided I would wait until it was finished before I researched and planned how to get it published.

When it was almost completed, I started doing my research on publishing and printing. I reached out to a couple of people that I know who have written books to get ideas on what steps to take. It all seemed to be above my head, and I was having trouble taking the next steps. But I knew without a doubt that this book is His plan for me, so I continued to trust Him to provide the people and the tools.

> *For He whom God has sent speaks the Words of God, for God does not give the Spirit by measure. John 3:34*

One Sunday morning right out of the blue I got a text from Lia, a lady from church, asking if I was going to church that day. It seemed her husband was going to be the speaker. I told her I would watch it online as I haven't gone in person often since the pandemic. She asked what I was up to that day and I told her I was in for the day and working on my book. She asked about the book. I told her the story behind why I was writing it and that I was almost done with the writing part. She responded by offering to edit the book for me as she worked as a copy editor for years. I see God's Hand in getting His work completed.

Five months later, I had not heard from Lia yet regarding the book as her schedule was quite full with family obligations. While praying about the book I decided to ask my friend/coworker to give read it over without editing just to give me her honest opinion. No one else had seen it before. A little more than a week later she told me that she thought it was really powerful, very personal, but powerful. She mentioned a few incidents in my life and asked why I did not touch on them. I explained that I did not want the book to be all about "Lisa's Dramas." I wanted it to be about where God equipped me, prepared me, held me, and rescued me. She agreed that I should indeed continue on to have it printed.

That same weekend at temple, Rabbi Joe gave a great message on "Waiting on the Lord." Our ladies group kept posting songs about "In the waiting." Two days later at 3:30 am I had given up the idea of falling asleep. I was watching a Hallmark movie and the remote stopped working. I turned the television off and back on again and it did not return to the Hallmark channel. It flipped on to a channel where Dr. Charles Stanley was giving a message on "Patience Essential" with the words "HAVE THE WILL TO WAIT" on the bottom of the screen. I heard, "God is your greatest protector, when He says no, He is not rejecting you, He is protecting you." So, I realized that I needed to just take my time with this book and wait on Him.

The following day I sat on my porch praying, singing, and talking to God. I went in the house and got the book and decided to read straight through it in its entirety without stopping to spell check or make changes, so that I could see if this book honored the Glory of the Lord and if the verses that I

171

chose were fitting to the stories. For two days I was either on my porch swing or in the house sitting on my stairway concentrating word for word. As I continued reading chapter after chapter, I had this powerful feeling of urgency and energy racing through me the entire time. I took breaks in between to eat, mop a floor, drop clothes in the washer and think as I worked. The second day at the bottom of my stairs I was feeling overwhelmed by His Presence as I finished the chapters and thought out loud to the Lord, "YES, this is about You and not me."

I then got on my computer and continued my research on publishing and printing. I went from website to website trying to understand how it worked, what an ISBN number is, what does font point size and graphic size mean? And I prayed, "Lord, You gave me this and I know this is for Your Glory. I wait on You and trust in You to help me understand how to get this into print." I was on the computer for two days.

I can't tell you if it was from the shoulder surgery or from the urgency of finding answers, but once again, I could not sleep at all. I gave up trying and turned on the television. There on the screen was Joel Osteen and he had Tyler Perry on giving the testimony of the struggles before his works became famous. He quoted his saying, "It doesn't matter if a million people tell you what you can't do, or if ten million tell you no. If you get one yes from God that's all you need." And he said, "God did not bring you this far to leave you." And then he pulled out his Bible and read ***Genesis 22:6-7***, ***"6 And Abraham took the wood of the burnt offering, and laid*** it ***upon Isaac his son; and he took the fire in his hand, and a knife; and they went both of them together. 7 And Isaac spake unto Abraham his father, and said, My father: and he said, Here*** am ***I, my son. And he said, Behold the fire and the wood: but where*** is ***the lamb for a burnt offering?***

172

This is the same verse that Pastor Stewart read to us on that Sunday morning in November of 2019 when God gave me the title of this book! No doubt about it, "He Cover's Me" is one of my burnt offerings, and if God brought me this far, He will help me complete the task with the perfect words to honor Him!

This is getting a little long, but bear with me, for when God is at the center, it is worth the wait! The next Sunday morning I rode with my neighbors to church service. It was only my third in-person service since the COVID-19 pandemic. The youth pastor was speaking and his message was right on point. He kept referring to someone else in the congregation who worked very hard over the years to learn graphic designing and many other achievements. His words that stayed with me were, "He never looked to the left or to the right, he just concentrated on the task at hand."

Two weeks later, I was listening to Rabbi Joe's message. His words were as bold as can be, so I took out my phone and typed, "Again, with the -Do not deviate to the left nor to the right, be bold and courageous to be successful."

Whenever I go to church, I usually sit in the same pew so I can see everything and I have space to jump up and worship without knocking someone over. Now sharing this pew is a beautiful Spirit-Filled woman, who has always greeted me with a welcoming hug (air hugs now with this pandemic). We often text each to say hello and share inspirational quotes. On my birthday, I was surprised to find a birthday card in the mailbox with a check in it! Honestly, I don't even know anything about her personal life, so I was surprised at the gift. I decided to put it away until the Lord put it in my heart what to do with it.

Chapter 20

In Closing

As I finish up the final chapter of this book, I consider how to end this. Every time I think I am finished I remember something else to write. The ending of this book is definitely not the ending of my story:

No one can tell me there is no God. The words can come out of their mouths, but they will never convince me. I have experienced His Mighty Presence too often to ever let go. I have witnessed answers to immediate prayer over and over again. I felt His arms wrap around me in the middle of a desperate lonely night that left me with the knowledge that I am NEVER alone!

I have felt His arms around me in the middle of my worship or prayers. Sometimes His Presence is so overwhelming in the middle of dancing during a service that I want drop to the ground right there, but I can't since I am on the dance ministry and assisting in leading the congregation. So, I will be right there in that circle with my arms up high with tears streaming down my face in adoration while I am dancing.

There are times when I am praying with my arms up in the air and I don't feel His Presence and I say to Him, "I know You are here, please let those in this room that don't know, but really need to know that You are here, feel Your Mighty Presence." And all of a sudden, His Presence will surround me overwhelmingly and I will just hug Him and cry and say, "Thank You, thank You, thank You!" He really loves to surprise us with blessings when we are praying for or giving to others. He loves a giving heart.

One time I was walking back and forth in the front row praying for the people that were standing at the altar, and I felt His Presence and the breeze of someone walking beside me. I looked down quickly to witness His sandaled foot walking beside me. Unfortunately, I lost it right then and there and His Presence left! I was so overwhelmed with His Presence that I started crying with overwhelming joy and my heart was racing wildly. I chased our special moment away. Then I told the Lord that I was sorry I got so excited and asked Him to let me not lose myself in those moments. I want to be strong and bask in His Presence.

If you have never felt His Presence here is some advice for you.

<u>Study His Word daily and adjust your life accordingly</u>: He will not be showing His Presence or blessing you if your ways are not in accordance with the standards that He has set for us. You cannot be living in the world without fear of the Lord or consideration of His instructions and expect blessings. We have consequences to our actions.

> *But seek first the kingdom of God and his righteousness, and all these things will be added to you.* <u>**Matthew 6:33**</u>

<u>Open your heart to accept that He is real and that He longs for you to feel His Presence</u>: You have to allow yourself to believe, truly believe, that He is real and He is able to do anything under the sun. Quiet yourself down and wait expectantly for His arms to wrap around you.

Glory in his holy name; let the hearts of those who seek the Lord rejoice! Seek the LORD and his strength; seek his Presence continually! Remember the wondrous works that he has done, his miracles and the judgments he uttered, <u>**1-Chronicles 16: 10-12**</u>

<u>Read your Bible and let it penetrate into your heart and soul</u>: Don't make the same mistake I did throughout my life by opening my Bible and reading it fast without concentrating on the meaning. Take your time and read little verses at a time, let the words sink in, then consider what they are saying to you.

Keep this Book of the Law always on your lips; meditate on it day and night, so that you may be careful to do everything written in it. Then you will be prosperous and successful. <u>**Joshua 1:8**</u>

<u>Share His love with others</u>: Sing to Him, dance with Him, speak of His blessings in your life, reach out to those around you and tell them how great our God is. When you are feeling sad and lonely, turn on the music in your room and sing and dance and praise Him. When your friend tells you that they feel like there is no hope, share that Hope in Him with them.

And He said to them, "Go into all the world and preach the gospel to all creation. He who has believed and has been baptized shall be saved; but he who has disbelieved shall be condemned. <u>**Mark 16:15-16**</u>

<u>Keep your eyes WIDE Open</u>: If you do not keep your eyes wide open at all times, you will miss some of the most beautiful encounters that He shares with us. Look up and see

His sky, His clouds, His stars, and His rainbows. Take time to see the majestic mountains and the powerful ocean. Take the time to watch the animals at play. Even the ants are known by God for their mighty strength. Take nothing for granted. If you are blessed with eyes that see clearly, then use them to observe His goodness. If your sight is poor, but your ears are good, then listen to His Word and sing worship songs. If you can dance, then dance with Him every day.

My most important message in this book is that He is with us every single day of our lives. He gives us every breath we take. He knows our innermost thoughts. He longs to share His Presence with you. In this book, as you hear of my life and how He was there every step of the way, I pray that somehow, it will help all who read this to know that HE is with them also- every step of the way.

The hardest day of my life was when I got that call to hear that my firstborn son was shot and killed. The second hardest was putting his beautiful body in that casket never to see that beautiful face again. However, God turned it all around and showered me with HIS Presence every step of my journey. He protected me and kept me strong. He provided me with angels both on earth and around me to keep me from falling.

These are just a few last-minute thoughts that I can share with you. I am amazed at how our Awesome God blesses me day after day after day. The more I do for others, the more He does for me. The more I tithe and share, the more He gives, the more I sing and dance praises to His Name, the more joy He puts in my heart.

This book it is all about loving and trusting our ABBA. It is about putting everything into HIS Mighty Hands and knowing without a doubt that HE's got this!

Those who know me know there was a "CRAZY Lisa" out there in my younger days. A Lisa that HAD to take all matters into her hands immediately -Rush in there like a BULL and save the day! Yea, that's it -save the day -or better yet say turn the world upside down. My heart was always racing.

I am saying this because there are still family members that just don't get it. I mean, they see me and how much my life has changed. I tell them to worship and give God the trust and their lives will be different, but they just can't seem to grasp it. But then again, would I have listened to anyone back then?

I just thank God that He is my best friend, my mother, my father, my comforter, my GOOGLE, my all in all. And you know what? My life is so beautiful. Yes, I could have more money in the bank, or a husband that liked to share romantic getaways, or my family could all be here with me. But no matter where I am or who I am with, I am good. I seek Him, and I act in accordance to how I think He would approve.

Try it my friends. Just take time daily to share with Him and ask Him if should you turn left, or right? Ask Him if you should find a new job or where to look. Ask Him to bless you with answers. and most importantly, *BELIEVE* that He will provide and that He is indeed listening.

My prayer is that as long as I breathe, I will remember who God is to me. In fact, I have told people close to me that if I get to the stage in my life where I do not remember anything including them and their place in my life, that the one thing I ask of them is to remind me of God every day. Don't sit and tell me who you are to me or what we have been through. Yes, my life and the people in it are all very important to me.

Make sure you sit with me every day and tell me who God is and how much God loves me. Tell me that every day so He will be my last thought as I leave this world.

ABBA, let the last breath I take be spent on You! In Yeshua's Mighty Name I pray-AMEN

With my whole heart I have sought You; oh, let me not wander from Your commandments! Your Word I have hidden in my heart, that I might not sin against You. Blessed are You, O LORD! Teach me Your statutes.
PSALM 119:10 –12

Special Side Note:

James Jr, Grandma loves you!

As I complete this I want to just send a shout out to James Jr, my teenage grandson. He asked me if he was in the book and I realized that I did not mention him. I told him that I just wrote a collection of stories that spoke out to me as to where God was in different circumstances.

So, I want to share a personal message to him. Jamie, Grandma Lisa adores you! I was there the day you were born. I held your tiny hand when the nurses weren't looking and I prayed over you. I called you Shlomo – which means God's Peace is with you. You are my first-born grandson who looks just like your daddy and also a lot like my daddy. I thank God for you daily. I will always be here for you! Never stop giving your best in all you do. You will do great things with your life! LOVE LOVE LOVE YOU!

Encourage ONE ANOTHER & BUILD EACH OTHER UP

· 1 Thessalonians 5:11 ·

He Covers Me

By Lisa Bryan

About the Author

Lisa Bryan is just an ordinary woman with extraordinary faith in GOD. Worship, prayer, praise, and dance is her life now. Her main goal is to encourage others daily to look to for God in all circumstances.

Her family composition is quite complicated. Simply put, Lisa is a wife, mother, stepmother, grandmother, sister, aunt, and friend. She also has her little nine-year-old Yorkie, Precious Godiva (meaning Beloved Gift of God).

Lisa describes her life as a roller-coaster of ups and mostly downs for many years until she finally made Yeshua her heart's desire. She has worked for over twenty-six years at an elderly housing facility. She is a member of Temple Aron Hakodesh (a messianic synagogue), and she also calls Pentecostal Tabernacle International her second church home. She serves on many ministries at temple. She asks the Lord daily, "What can I do for you, ABBA?" This is the answer she received one day, "Where is your burnt offering?

"He Covers Me" is her very first attempt at writing a book. Since she could pick up a pen. she has had a passion to write her feelings down either in a journal, a song, or a poem. Though she excelled in school, she never took any courses in writing or publishing. This book, through a huge leap of faith, is that Burnt Offering.